W9-BTO-969

Open Government:
An American Tradition Faces National Security, Privacy, and Other Challenges

POINT COUNTERPOINT

Affirmative Action
Amateur Athletics
American Military Policy
Animal Rights
Capital Punishment
DNA Evidence
Election Reform
Freedom of Speech
Gay Rights
Gun Control
Immigration Policy
Legalizing Marijuana
Mandatory Military Service
Mental Health Reform
Open Government
Physician-Assisted Suicide
Policing the Internet
Religion in Public Schools
Rights of Students
Search and Seizure
Smoking Bans
The FCC and Regulating Indecency
The Right to Privacy
Trial of Juveniles as Adults
The War on Terror
Welfare Reform

Open Government:
An American Tradition Faces National Security, Privacy, and Other Challenges

David L. Hudson, Jr.

SERIES CONSULTING EDITOR
Alan Marzilli, M.A., J.D.

CHELSEA HOUSE PUBLISHERS
A Haights Cross Communications Company

Philadelphia

CHELSEA HOUSE PUBLISHERS

VP, NEW PRODUCT DEVELOPMENT   Sally Cheney
DIRECTOR OF PRODUCTION   Kim Shinners
CREATIVE MANAGER   Takeshi Takahashi
MANUFACTURING MANAGER   Diann Grasse

Staff for OPEN GOVERNMENT

EXECUTIVE EDITOR   Lee Marcott
ASSISTANT EDITOR   Alexis Browsh
PHOTO EDITOR   Sarah Bloom
PRODUCTION EDITOR   Noelle Nardone
SERIES AND COVER DESIGNER   Keith Trego
LAYOUT   21st Century Publishing and Communications, Inc.

Library of Congress Cataloging-in-Publication Data

Hudson, David L., 1969–
    Open government: an American tradition faces national security, privacy, and other challenges / David L. Hudson, Jr.
        p. cm.—(Point/counterpoint)
Includes bibliographical references.
    ISBN 0-7910-8090-0 (hardcover)
    1. Freedom of information—United States. 2. National security—United States. 3. Privacy, Right of—United States. 4. Transparency in government—United States. I. Title. II. Point-counterpoint (Philadelphia, Pa.)
JC598.H83 2005
323.44'8'0973—dc22

                                                                    2004022047

CONTENTS

Foreword

Alan Marzilli, M.A., J.D.
Durham, North Carolina

The debates presented in POINT/COUNTERPOINT are among the most interesting and controversial in contemporary American society, but studying them is more than an academic activity. They affect every citizen; they are the issues that today's leaders debate and tomorrow's will decide. The reader may one day play a central role in resolving them.

Why study both sides of the debate? It's possible that the reader will not yet have formed any opinion at all on the subject of this volume—but this is unlikely. It is more likely that the reader will already hold an opinion, probably a strong one, and very probably one formed without full exposure to the arguments of the other side. It is rare to hear an argument presented in a balanced way, and it is easy to form an opinion on too little information; these books will help to fill in the informational gaps that can never be avoided. More important, though, is the practical function of the series: Skillful argumentation requires a thorough knowledge of *both* sides—though there are seldom only two, and only by knowing what an opponent is likely to assert can one form an articulate response.

Perhaps more important is that listening to the other side sometimes helps one to see an opponent's arguments in a more human way. For example, Sister Helen Prejean, one of the nation's most visible opponents of capital punishment, has been deeply affected by her interactions with the families of murder victims. Seeing the families' grief and pain, she understands much better why people support the death penalty, and she is able to carry out her advocacy with a greater sensitivity to the needs and beliefs of those who do not agree with her. Her relativism, in turn, lends credibility to her work. Dismissing the other side of the argument as totally without merit can be too easy—it is far more useful to understand the nature of the controversy and the reasons *why* the issue defies resolution.

The most controversial issues of all are often those that center on a constitutional right. The Bill of Rights—the first ten amendments to the U.S. Constitution—spells out some of the most fundamental rights that distinguish the governmental system of the United States from those that allow fewer (or other) freedoms. But the sparsely worded document is open to interpretation, and clauses of only a few words are often at the heart of national debates. The Bill of Rights was meant to protect individual liberties; but the needs of some individuals clash with those of society as a whole, and when this happens someone has to decide where to draw the line. Thus the Constitution becomes a battleground between the rights of individuals to do as they please and the responsibility of the government to protect its citizens. The First Amendment's guarantee of "freedom of speech," for example, leads to a number of difficult questions. Some forms of expression, such as burning an American flag, lead to public outrage—but nevertheless are said to be protected by the First Amendment. Other types of expression that most people find objectionable, such as sexually explicit material involving children, are not protected because they are considered harmful. The question is not only where to draw the line, but how to do this without infringing on the personal liberties on which the United States was built.

The Bill of Rights raises many other questions about individual rights and the societal "good." Is a prayer before a high school football game an "establishment of religion" prohibited by the First Amendment? Does the Second Amendment's promise of "the right to bear arms" include concealed handguns? Is stopping and frisking someone standing on a corner known to be frequented by drug dealers a form of "unreasonable search and seizure" in violation of the Fourth Amendment? Although the nine-member U.S. Supreme Court has the ultimate authority in interpreting the Constitution, its answers do not always satisfy the public. When a group of nine people—sometimes by a five-to-four vote—makes a decision that affects the lives of hundreds of millions, public outcry can be expected. And the composition of the Court does change over time, so even a landmark decision is not guaranteed to stand forever. The limits of constitutional protection are always in flux.

These issues make headlines, divide courts, and decide elections. They are the questions most worthy of national debate, and this series aims to cover them as thoroughly as possible. Each volume sets out some of the key arguments surrounding a particular issue, even some views that most people consider extreme or radical—but presents a balanced perspective on the issue. Excerpts from the relevant laws and judicial opinions and references to central concepts, source material, and advocacy groups help the reader to explore the issues even further and to read "the letter of the law" just as the legislatures and the courts have established it.

It may seem that some debates—such as those over capital punishment and abortion, debates with a strong moral component—will never be resolved. But American history offers numerous examples of controversies that once seemed insurmountable but now are effectively settled, even if only on the surface. Abolitionists met with widespread resistance to their efforts to end slavery, and the controversy over that issue threatened to cleave the nation in two; but today public debate over the merits of slavery would be unthinkable, though racial inequalities still plague the nation. Similarly unthinkable at one time was suffrage for women and minorities, but this is now a matter of course. Distributing information about contraception once was a crime. Societies change, and attitudes change, and new questions of social justice are raised constantly while the old ones fade into irrelevancy.

Whatever the root of the controversy, the books in POINT/ COUNTERPOINT seek to explain to the reader the origins of the debate, the current state of the law, and the arguments on both sides. The goal of the series is to inform the reader about the issues facing not only American politicians, but all of the nation's citizens, and to encourage the reader to become more actively involved in resolving these debates, as a voter, a concerned citizen, a journalist, an activist, or an elected official. Democracy is based on education, and every voice counts—so every opinion must be an informed one.

This volume looks at the controversy over how much information Americans should be able to obtain about their government, including the court system. After an era in which the press and the public had much greater insight into the workings of the government, the "age of terror" has led to greater restrictions, and many people fear that these restrictions will lead to dire consequences. U.S. Congressman John Moss, who opposed the government's growing secrecy during the "cold war" with the Soviet Union in the 1950s and 1960s, left an important legacy. His efforts led to the passage of the Freedom of Information Act, or FOIA, a 1966 federal law allowing people to access government documents. However, the law contains exceptions, and the Homeland Security Act, passed in the wake of the 9/11 terrorist attacks, has broadened those exemptions. The war on terror has led to other types of secrecy, with the government arguing that it must conduct closed proceedings against terrorists and limit reporters' access to the battlefield. However, many question how the public can ensure that the military is acting fairly under such circumstances. Other developments have raised other concerns about access to information. Cable networks devoted to televising trials, some fear, disrupt the court system. Others believe that the growing problem of identity theft justifies limits on access to government records containing private information about citizens. This volume provides a concise overview of the legal basis of open government, as well as the issues that courts face in balancing open government against security, civil rights, and privacy concerns.

The Place of Open Government in America

A popular Government without popular information or the means of acquiring it, is but a Prologue to a Farce or a Tragedy or perhaps both. Knowledge will forever govern ignorance, and a people who mean to be their own Governors, must arm themselves with the power knowledge gives.

—James Madison, 1822

James Madison, the primary author of the First Amendment, wrote these words in 1822 in a letter to W.T. Barry to express his view that the people must "arm themselves with the power knowledge gives." These words have come to symbolize the mantra, or slogan, of this country's mandate of an open government.

The Constitution begins with the words "We the People." It is the people who are supposed to retain the ultimate power. In a constitutional democracy, the people must have access to the government. They must be able to have the means of acquiring information about governmental activities.

Open government means that the people may acquire information about governmental activities. This is done through at least two types of laws: open records laws and open meeting laws. Open records laws provide that many types of public documents must be available for inspection and copying by and for requesting individuals. Open meeting laws, or sunshine laws as they are often called, ensure that many governmental bodies conduct their meetings in public.

In our system of federalism, we have a federal government and various state governments. With federal and state laws. In the area of open government, we have federal open records and open meetings laws. We have the same pattern in the states. Keep in mind that in our system of government, each state enacts its own statutes. This means that the open records laws of California and Tennessee will differ.

All of these laws, however, are designed to follow James Madison's basic principle—that the people have a means to acquire information about their government. Only then can the United States of America be a fully functioning constitutional democracy. This belief in open government sparked former California Congressman John Moss to pursue diligently for more than a decade the passage of a federal law called the Freedom of Information Act, or FOIA. Belief in open government caused attorney and investigator Allan Favish to pursue information about the government investigations into the declared suicide death of former White House counsel Vince Foster. Belief in open government has caused many freedom-of-information advocates to question government policy in the war on terrorism.

Suffice it to say that, in today's world, there are many controversies about open government, particularly in the age of terrorism. The government, in its attempt to combat terrorism, has had to withdraw some information from public view. Obviously, combating terrorism is a most compelling governmental goal. As attorney and author Al Knight has written, "The first job of law is to provide freedom from violence and the fear of violence that kills civilization at its roots. Until that job is done, nothing else about a legal system works."[1]

In 2002, Congress passed the Homeland Security Act. Part of that law, called the Critical Infrastructure Information Act of 2002, allows private entities to give information to the government about critical infrastructure in exchange for secrecy and immunity from lawsuits. Infrastructure means the basic structure or features of a system or organization. Section 204 of the measure provides: "Information provided voluntarily by non-Federal entities or individuals that relates to infrastructure vulnerabilities or other vulnerabilities to terrorism and is or has been in the possession of the Department shall not be subject to section 552 of title 5, United States Code." This means that the information is not subject to the Freedom of Information Act (FOIA).

The measure also criminalizes government agency disclosures of certain critical infrastructure information. This means that even those government workers who release the information for the common good, such as those who expose wrongdoing (called whistleblowers), can be punished. This measure caused Senator Patrick Leahy to say the act was "the most severe weakening of the Freedom of Information Act in its 36-year history."[2] Leahy and others introduced the Restoration of Freedom of Information Act of 2003, designed to take some of the sting out of the new law.[3]

Some believe that the government has gone too far in the War on Terror and threatened the viability of an open government. "More than one reporter has quipped that the War on Terrorism might as well be renamed the War on Reporters or on the public's right to know," wrote *Los Angeles Times* writer Josh Meyer. He further noted, "Most would concur that no matter how the courts are ruling, the Justice Department and the FBI essentially have blocked the release of virtually every scrap of information that reporters need to do their jobs."[4]

Open government laws under scrutiny

Five out of 15 states considering tighter laws on freedom of information have already passed measures limiting access to documents or meetings. Twenty-one states passed such laws last year.

Considering revision of open government laws

Have passed laws tightening public access

SOURCE: Associated Press   AP

Open government is part of the foundation of the United States, but in recent years some have suggested tightening freedom of information laws in the interest of national security. This map shows states that are considering laws or have already passed laws restricting public access to government information.

The question becomes where to draw the line in a free society with the goal of protecting society in a tradition of open government. The challenge is daunting. The ideal of open government, however, extends far beyond access of information for reporters in a post-9/11 world. They include many other issues, such as:

- whether the media's free-press rights and the public right to know are threatened by the closing of access in numerous high-profile trials

- whether the increased use of sealing court documents and the use of alternative dispute resolutions threaten the public's right to know about important court cases

- whether cameras should be used to televise court proceedings

- whether the public should have access to 9-1-1 emergency telephone calls

- whether the public should have access to autopsy photographs

- whether the press should have right of access to prisons, military bases, and other restricted areas

- whether the government should be able to withhold the names of the detainees held in the wake of the 9/11 investigation

- whether the government should be able to close "special interest" immigration hearings across the board

- whether the vice president must disclose the details of an energy taskforce meeting under the federal open meetings law called the Federal Advisory Committee Act

- whether state education departments must release the social security numbers of teachers

With respect to the media's free-press rights and the public's right to know (the first example listed above), judges in numerous high-profile cases have denied access to the media, closed their courtrooms, allowed anonymous juries (juries in which the identities of the jurors are kept secret), and taken other measures that seem to advance secrecy. For example, celebrity Martha Stewart won her right to be tried by an anonymous jury. In the sexual assault case involving basketball star Kobe Bryant, a Colorado judge banned cameras and sealed many records. A California judge barred cameras from much of the murder trial of actor Robert Blake. Another California judge imposed gag orders—judicial orders that call for trial participants or even the press to be silent—on the attorneys in the criminal case of pop singer Michael Jackson. The judge in the Scott Peterson case sealed juror questionnaires, banned all cameras from the courtroom, and issued a gag order on all trial participants.[5]

These issues merit full discussion in a society committed to an open government, and this book examines four "open government" controversies:

(1) whether cameras should be permitted in courtrooms;

(2) whether the Freedom of Information Act's privacy exemptions properly balance open government versus privacy;

(3) whether the press should have right of access to the battlefield; and

(4) whether the government is striking a proper balance between open access and security during the Age of Terror.

The book further examines the efforts of people like Congressman John Moss to pass a federal freedom-of-information law. It discusses the case of Allan Favish and his efforts to obtain information from the U.S. government about the death of Vince Foster. It discusses whether the government should have the power to conduct a form of secret justice in cases involving those with alleged ties to terrorists and in other legal proceedings.

Privacy Rights Often Must Trump the Free Flow of Information

An individual's interest in controlling the dissemination of information regarding personal matters does not dissolve simply because that information may be available to the public in some form.

—U.S. Supreme Court Justice Clarence Thomas in *United States Department of Defense* v. *Federal Labor Relations Authority* (1994).

On February 18, 2001, auto racing legend Dale Earnhardt died after a crash during the Daytona 500 race. His death was a tragedy to his family, friends, colleagues, and millions of fans. After his death, the media wanted access to his autopsy photographs. Dale's widow, Teresa Earnhardt, considered it a privacy and dignity issue. She did not believe the press should be allowed to publish photographs of her dead husband. Teresa Earnhardt believed in the sanctity of privacy, and she fought for it. As a result, Florida and several others states changed their laws to prohibit prying into photographs that should remain private. The press and the public have important First Amendment rights, but those rights are not unfettered. People should retain the right to privacy, or what Supreme Court justices Louis Brandeis and Samuel Warren called the right of privacy or right to be "let alone." [1]

The Freedom of Information Act provides for a policy of disclosure to ensure that the public can keep track of the government. Even President Johnson recognized privacy interests when he signed FOIA into law. He stated:

> Fairness to individuals also requires that information accumulated in personnel files be protected from disclosure. Officials within government must be able to communicate with one another fully and frankly without publicity. They cannot operate effectively if required to disclose information prematurely or to make public investigative files and internal instructions that guide them in arriving at their decisions. [2]

FOIA, however, contains specific exemptions that seek to ensure privacy. Exemption 6 prohibits the disclosure of "personnel and medical files and similar files the disclosure of which would constitute a clearly unwarranted invasion of personal privacy." [3]

Exemption 7(C) of FOIA provides that the government does not have to release "records or information compiled for law enforcement purposes" if the release of such information "could reasonably be expected to constitute an unwarranted invasion of personal privacy." [4]

The U.S. Supreme Court Has a History of Protecting Privacy Interests in FOIA Cases

The U.S. Supreme Court has addressed several freedom-of-information requests that affect these privacy interests. Often, the Court has determined that information falls within privacy exemptions. In one case, the U.S. Supreme Court also determined that FOIA did not compel federal agencies to disclose the home addresses of its employees to two local labor unions. In *U.S. Dept. of Defense* v. *Federal Labor Relations Authority*, the U.S. Supreme Court ruled that the federal agencies could withhold this information under Exemption 6.[5] The labor unions argued that the information would not constitute a "clearly unwarranted invasion of personal privacy" because much of the information was already in the public domain and available through telephone books and voter registration lists.

The Supreme Court rejected this argument by the labor unions and affirmed privacy interests. "An individual's interest in controlling the dissemination of information regarding personal matters does not dissolve simply because that information may be available to the public in some form," the Court wrote. "Many people simply do not want to be disturbed at home by work-related matters. . . . We are reluctant to disparage the privacy interest of the home, which is accorded special consideration in our Constitution, laws, and traditions."[6]

In 2004, the U.S. Supreme Court reaffirmed its strong commitment to privacy, even in the face of FOIA requests, in the case of *National Archives and Records Administration* v. *Favish.*[7] Allan Favish was formerly the associate counsel for a group called Accuracy in Media, which had petitioned the government for the death-scene photographs of Vince Foster, the former White House deputy counsel to President Bill Clinton. Foster had died of a gunshot wound to the head in 1993. Government investigators concluded that his death was a suicide, but Favish was not convinced. He questioned whether Foster's death was really a suicide and suspected some sort of government concealment.

Favish was skeptical of the government's investigations and sought the photographs to show that these investigations were incomplete, incompetent, or untrustworthy. The government agencies, first the National Park Service and then the National Archives and Records Administration, countered that they did not have to release the information to Favish because of the privacy interests of Foster's family.

Favish countered that FOIA exemption 7(C) did not extend to the privacy interests of a deceased person's family members. He also argued that even if there was such a privacy interest, the public's right to know prevailed over privacy.

The U.S. Supreme Court unanimously sided with the government. First, the Court determined that the concept of privacy in the statute encompassed family members' interest in personal privacy. Justice Anthony Kennedy noted that the Foster family "seek to be shielded by the exemption to secure their own refuge from a sensation-seeking culture for their own peace of mind and tranquility, not for the sake of the deceased."[8] The Court also noted that traditionally both common law (cases from various courts) and statutory law supported the right of family members to control the body of the deceased "and to limit attempts to exploit pictures of the deceased family member's remains for public purposes."[9]

The government argued that FOIA requests are often made by criminals seeking autopsies, photos, and records of their deceased victims. The Court cited this as evidence that there is often strong reason for failure to disclose such information. The Court concluded, "FOIA recognizes surviving family members' right to personal privacy with respect to their close relative's death-scene images."[10]

Next, the Court proceeded to the balancing of interests between privacy and disclosure of information. The Court established the following test:

> Where the privacy concerns addressed by Exemption 7(C) are present, the exemption requires the person requesting the information to establish a sufficient reason for the disclosure. First, the citizen must show that the public interest sought to be advanced is a significant one, an interest more specific than having the information for its own sake. Second, the citizen must show the information is likely to advance that interest. Otherwise, the invasion of privacy is unwarranted.[11]

Applying this test, the government determined that Favish could not show that the death-scene photographs of Vince Foster would advance his theory that the government's investigations were improper. "Favish has not produced any evidence that would warrant a belief by a reasonable person that the alleged Government impropriety might have occurred to put the balance into play," the Court wrote.[12]

Concern for privacy had also led to another victory for privacy-rights advocates in the U.S. Supreme Court several years earlier. In 1989, the U.S. Supreme Court ruled in *United States Department of Justice* v. *Reporters Committee for Freedom of the Press* that the government could legally refuse to disclose FBI "rap sheets" to members of the press.[13]

The Reporters Committee for Freedom of the Press sought FBI rap sheets, detailing the criminal histories of four members of a family allegedly connected to organized crime in Pennsylvania. The family's company had allegedly obtained a number of defense contracts because of an improper bargain with a corrupt member of Congress.

A federal district court denied the request, but a federal appeals court reversed the decision. The appeals court determined that an individual's privacy interest in criminal history information contained in public records was minimal.

The case went to the U.S. Supreme Court. The FBI argued that the rap sheets could be withheld under Exemption 7 of the Freedom of Information Act. The Reporters Committee countered that the rap sheet in question did not implicate privacy interests because it was a compilation of materials gleaned from various public records. The Supreme Court sided with the FBI, noting that most states did not provide public access to criminal history summaries of individuals. "In sum, the fact that an 'event is not wholly private' does not mean that an individual has no interest in limiting disclosure or dissemination of the information," the Court wrote.[14] The Court also noted that the information sought by the Reporters Committee was not about the government but information about a private citizen.

State Courts Also Respect Privacy Exemptions to Open Records Requests

As mentioned in the previous chapter, every state has an open records law and an open meetings law designed to keep the public in the know about government actions. State legislatures

FROM THE BENCH

U.S. Dept. of Justice v. Reporters Committee for Freedom of the Press (1989)

What we have said should make clear that the public interest in the release of any rap sheet on Medico that may exist is not the type of interest protected by the FOIA.... If respondents are entitled to have the FBI tell them what it knows about Medico's criminal history, any other member of the public is entitled to the same disclosure—whether for writing a news story, for deciding whether to employ Medico, to rent a house to him, to extend credit to him, or simply to confirm or deny a suspicion. There is unquestionably, some public interest in providing interested citizens with answers to their questions about Medico. But that interest falls outside the ambit of the public interest that the FOIA was enacted to serve.

Finally: The privacy interest in maintaining the practical obscurity of rap-sheet information will always be high. When the subject of such a rap sheet is a private citizen and when the information is in the Government's control as a compilation, rather than as a record of "what the Government is up to," the privacy interest protected by Exemption 7(C) is in fact at its apex while the FOIA-based public interest in disclosure is at its nadir. Such a disparity on the scales of justice holds for a class of cases without regard to individual circumstances: the standard virtues of bright-line rules are thus present, and the difficulties attendant to ad-hoc adjudication may be avoided. Accordingly, we hold as a categorical matter that a third party's request for law enforcement records or information about a private citizen can reasonably be expected to invade that citizen's privacy, and that when the request seeks no 'official information' about a Government agency, but merely records that the Government happens to be storing, the invasion of privacy is "unwarranted."

and courts also recognize that privacy rights often trump the public's right to know.

Perhaps the best example of this concerns the Dale Earnhardt autopsy photo case mentioned at the beginning of the chapter. After Earnhardt's tragic death, an autopsy was performed on his body pursuant to state law. Additionally, 33 photographs were taken during the autopsy.

The Orlando Sentinel, Campus Communications, and others filed requests for the photographs. Earnhardt's wife Teresa, however, had sought an emergency court order prohibiting release of the photographs. A trial judge granted Mrs. Earnhardt's request. A month later, the Florida legislature passed a law that closed autopsy photographs from public view.

THE LETTER OF THE LAW

Chapter 2001-1, § 2 at 2, Laws of Florida

The Legislature finds that it is a public necessity that photographs and video and audio recordings of an autopsy be made confidential and exempt from the requirements of section 119.701(1), Florida Statutes, and Section 24(a) of Article I of the State Constitution. The Legislature finds that photographs or video or audio recordings of an autopsy depict or describe the deceased nude, bruised, bloodied, broken, with bullet or other wounds, cut open, dismembered, or decapitated. As such, photographs or video or audio recordings of an autopsy are highly sensitive depictions or descriptions of the deceased, as well as injury to the memory of the deceased. The Legislature notes that the existence of the World Wide Web and the proliferation of personal computers throughout the world encourages and promotes the wide dissemination of photographs and video and audio recordings would subject the immediate family of the deceased to continuous injury. The Legislature further notes that there continue to be other types of available information, such as the autopsy report, which are less intrusive and injurious to the immediate family members of the deceased and which continue to provide for public oversight. The Legislature further finds that the exemption provided in this act should be given retroactive application because it is remedial in nature.

A trial judge upheld the constitutionality of the law, finding that the law advanced strong privacy interests. A Florida appeals court affirmed the trial court's ruling in favor of the law in *Campus Communications, Inc. v. Earnhardt.*[15]

A student newspaper asserted the law was overly broad because it prohibited all photos—even those that are not gruesome or traumatic. The appeals court disagreed, finding that the statute was narrowly drawn. The appeals court reasoned that the newspaper could obtain needed information from the written autopsy report, which remained open to the public. The court concluded: "It is also a declared constitutional principle that every individual has a right of privacy, and while our constitution does not catalogue every matter that one can hold as private, autopsy photographs which display the remains of a deceased human being is certainly one of them."[16]

Both the Florida Supreme Court and the United States Supreme Court declined to review the Florida appeals court ruling. Other states have passed similar laws.

Summary

"While technology can make access to electronically stored information faster and cheaper, it can also make invasions of personal privacy far easier."[17] Thus, in this day and age, the government must be afforded some leeway in determining what information is appropriate to release to the public. As one commentator has explained, "The reality of our new homeland security situation prompts sacrifices such as more deference for FOIA exemptions."[18]

Freedom of Information Is a Paramount Value Serving a Powerful Public Interest

The real security of a nation is the intelligence and understanding of its people. Every effort should be made by government—the servant and not the master—to assure that maximum information be available to the people who are the ultimate power under the Constitution.

—John Moss (U.S. Congressman considered to be the father of the Freedom of Information Act)

Freedom of information is a vital part of society. It not only helps increase public knowledge but it can increase public safety. In the 1970s, the Center for Auto Safety was instrumental—through FOIA requests—in shedding light on the dangers of certain steel-belted radial tires. The consumer group's persistence with FOIA was at least partially responsible for a massive recall of tires manufactured by Firestone, a recall that probably saved lives. Without the Freedom of Information Act, the actions by the Center for Auto Safety may never have been as effective. Before FOIA, public access was even more limited.

The Establishment of a Statutory Right to Information

In 1946, Congress passed the Administrative Procedure Act. Section 3 of the act provided for the release of information by federal government agencies. A Senate Judiciary Committee report declared that the theory of the law was that "administrative operations and procedures are public property which the general public, rather than a few specialists or lobbyists," should know. The law, however, gave government agencies broad authority to determine whether to publish government records. It allowed agencies to withhold information that required "secrecy in the public interest" or information "required for good cause to be confidential." "In sum, the section provided government agencies with a shield for virtually any withholding of public records that they might wish to make."[1]

Twenty years later, in 1966, President Lyndon Johnson reluctantly signed an amendment to the Administrative Procedure Act. Known as the Freedom of Information Act, or FOIA, this new law arose out of general opposition to the growing government secrecy that developed during the cold war. During this time, the government extended the national security classification system and expanded, as well, the executive privilege doctrine to keep information secret. Additionally, the federal government had grown tremendously, and this had led to more people being directly affected by actions conducted by the federal government and its agencies. Finally, many members of the news media increasingly had difficulty obtaining information from the government. As one treatise on freedom of information law explained, "The increasing tendency to secrecy in government thus came head-to-head with an increased demand for government information."[2]

In 1957, Representative John Moss of California introduced a measure that would create greater public accountability and freedom of information. His efforts would eventually lead to what became known as the Freedom of Information Act, which President Johnson signed into law on July 4, 1966.

Statement of Honorable John E. Moss, Congressional Record, June 20, 1966

Mr. Speaker, our system of government is based on the participation of the government, and as our population grows in numbers it is essential that it also grow in knowledge and understanding. We must remove every barrier to information about—and understanding of—Government activities consistent with our security if the American public is to be adequately equipped to fulfill the ever more demanding role of responsible citizenship.

S. 1160 is a bill which will accomplish that objective by shoring up the public right of access to the facts of government, and inherently, providing easier access to the officials clothed with governmental responsibility. S. 1160 will grant any person the right of access to official records of the Federal Government and most important, by far the more important, is the fact that this bill provides for judicial review of the refusal of access and the withholding of information. It is the device which expands the rights of the citizens and which protects them against arbitrary or capricious denials.

Mr. Speaker, let me reassure those few who may have doubts as to the wisdom of this legislation that the committee has, with the utmost sense of responsibility, attempted to achieve a balance between a public need to know and a necessary restraint upon access to information in specific instances. The bill lists nine categories of Federal documents which may be withheld to protect the national security or permit effective operation of the Government but the burden of proof to justify withholding is put upon the Federal agencies. S. 1160 is a moderate bill and carefully worked out. The measure is not intended to impinge upon the appropriate power of the Executive or to harass the agencies of Government. We are simply attempting—to enforce a basic public right—the right to access to Government information.

Available online at *http://www.johnemossfoundation.org/foi/cr_JEM.htm*.

When President Johnson signed the bill into law on July 4, 1966, he stated, "This legislation springs from one of our most essential principles: A democracy works best when the people have all the information that the security of the nation permits. No one should be able to pull curtains of secrecy around decisions which can be revealed without injury to the public interest."[3] He added that freedom of information is so important "that only the national security, not the desire of public officials or private citizens, should determine when it must be restricted."[4]

The basis of FOIA is that records of federal governmental agencies are accessible by the public unless covered by a specific exemption. In the words of the U.S. Supreme Court, "disclosure, not secrecy, is the dominant objective of the Act."[5] FOIA provides that federal agencies must disclose much of their business in a publication called *The Federal Register*. They must also make records available for public viewing and copying. Finally, agencies must release records when they receive a request from "any person." The act provides in relevant part:

> Except with respect to the records made available under paragraphs (1) and (2) of this subsection, and except as provided in subparagraph (E), each agency, **upon any request for records** which Reasonably describes such records and Is made in accordance with published rules stating the time, place, fees (if any), and procedures to be followed, shall make the records promptly available to **any person.**[6]

In the eyes of those concerned with the public's right to know, Attorney General John Ashcroft took a dangerous step in October 2001. He issued a memorandum on October 12, 2001 that placed more emphasis on the privacy and the other exemptions in FOIA. The attorney general gave lip service to the principle that FOIA ensures a well-informed citizenry, but then he added: "The Department of Justice and this Administration are equally committed to protecting other fundamental values

Quotable: Professor David C. Vladeck

The 1966 Freedom of Information Act (FOIA) is arguably the most important tool Americans have to oversee the workings of their government. FOIA was designed to bring an end to the idea that government could operate behind closed doors. FOIA establishes a presumption that all government information is available to the public, subject only to a few, narrowly circumscribed exemptions. Some information—agency rules and final orders and decisions—must be published and disseminated by the agency, and under newly added provisions of FOIA, agencies must make this information available over the Internet. But the heart of FOIA is its requirement that agencies, upon request, disclose any record in the agency's possession to anyone.[7]

that are held by our society. Among them are safeguarding our national security, enhancing the effectiveness of our law enforcement agencies, protecting sensitive business information and, not least, preserving personal privacy."[8] Ashcroft instructed the heads of all federal departments to release information under FOIA only "after full and deliberate consideration of the institutional, commercial, and personal privacy interests that could be implicated by disclosure of the information."[9]

Arguably, the greatest danger to the public's right to know comes from a greater societal recognition of privacy rights. According to a government study released in 2003, privacy was the top reason given by federal agencies for denying FOIA requests. These requests were denied under Exemptions 6 and 7(C). "While we were focusing on September 11, one thing that continued to grow was the use of the privacy exemption," said Charles Davis, executive director of the Freedom of Information Center at the University of Missouri.[10]

In its first case examining Exemption 6 of FOIA, the U.S. Supreme Court rejected the privacy rationale. The case, *Department of Air Force* v. *Rose*, involved an FOIA request by the *New York University Law Review* for records of Air Force Academy cadets accused of ethics code violations. The law student publication sought the information for an article on military disciplinary proceedings. In rejecting the application of Exemption 6 in the case, Justice William Brennan wrote: "Exemption 6 does not protect against disclosure every incidental invasion of privacy—only such disclosures that constitute 'clearly unwarranted' invasions of personal privacy." [11]

Unfortunately, the U.S. Supreme Court has placed greater emphasis on personal privacy than on the public's right to know. As mentioned in the previous chapter, attorney Allan Favish lost his FOIA suit seeking the release of photographs of former White House lawyer Vince Foster. The Supreme Court determined that the photos did not have to be released to Favish because of a privacy exemption in FOIA. As Justice Anthony Kennedy wrote for the Court, "Family members have a personal stake in honoring and mourning their dead and objecting to unwarranted public exploitation that, by intruding upon their own grief, tends to degrade the rights and respect they seek to accord to the deceased person who was once their own."

First Amendment advocates said the ruling could have damaging effects. Ken Paulson, the former executive director of the First Amendment Center, wrote that the "decision could have a longer shadow." [12] Veteran U.S. Supreme Court reporter Tony Mauro said, "The public should be very concerned about what the ruling could mean for the future." [13] Mauro warned that the Court's decision in the Vince Foster photo case means that family members could now stop the release of important government documents about their loved ones despite the public interest in the material. He added:

> Advocates of the right to know are hoping against hope that the impact of the Supreme Court's ruling can be confined to rare cases such as Foster's in which graphic death-scene photographs are at issue. They may be successful, but there

is enough language in the ruling to give aid and comfort to government officials whose first instinct is to close, not open, files.[14]

> • Do you think family members' privacy interests should trump information about government investigations?
> • Should Favish have won the right to view the death-scene photographs?

The ruling was tough for many open-government advocates to swallow because the Court set a high bar for those wishing to obtain law enforcement records. The Court denied Favish's request in part because he had not established any evidence that there was any government wrongdoing. As open-government advocate Rebecca Daugherty wrote, "Could it come to the point

Quotable: Ken Paulson

By expanding the definition of personal privacy, the Supreme Court has given government officials much broader grounds on which to deny requests for law enforcement records. The decision tips the balance in favor of privacy and against the free flow of information.

The ruling also tips the scales against citizens seeking to challenge their government. The Foster case has been much discussed on talk radio over the past decade. Despite the five investigations, some people believe that Foster's death was not a suicide. Of course, if you believe a government conspiracy was in place, you're not exactly comforted by the fact that five government agencies declared there was no such conspiracy. With this ruling, the Supreme Court is in essence saying, "The documents you're seeking to prove your case may not be released to you unless you do a better job of proving your case." This stance has implications for matters well beyond the Foster probe.

Source: Ken Paulson, "Supreme Court Places a Premium on Privacy," First Amendment Center Online. 4/1/04. Available online at: *http://www.firstamendmentcenter.org/commentary.aspx?id=13104.*

that you can't find out if anything is wrong unless you can show, to the government's satisfaction, that something is probably wrong?"[15]

Summary

In its 2004 *Favish* decision, the U.S. Supreme Court made it even harder to obtain FOIA information. The Court showed, once again, a strong sensitivity to privacy rights. The Court's decision was even more disturbing to many FOIA advocates because the privacy rights were not those of the person or persons identified in the records but the privacy rights of families. The Court said: "They seek to be shielded by the exemption to secure their own refuge from a sensation-seeking culture for their own peace of mind and tranquility."[16]

The Court's decision brought to bear the words of the Reporters Committee for Freedom of the Press, which had warned the Court in its amicus brief in support of Favish:

> Accordingly, the government's rule would turn the FOIA on its head, transforming a statute that is supposed to ensure disclosure subject to limited exceptions into a statute that, in a significant category of cases, ensures government secrecy and public ignorance. Such a rule, with consequences reaching far beyond the facts of this case, would prevent journalists from exposing government waste or fraud; it would prevent writers and historians from exposing and anatomizing past government wrongdoing; it would prevent analysts from assessing the success or failure of the government's initiatives; and it would prevent the public in general from finding out what its government is up to.[17]

Public Information Concerns Must Give Way to Security in a Post-9/11 World

We will not convert the First Amendment right of access to criminal judicial proceedings into a requirement that the government disclose information compiled during the exercise of a quintessential executive power—the investigation and prevention of terrorism.[1]

—Federal Appeals Court Judge David B. Sentelle, 2003

The terrorist attack of September 11, 2001, changed the equation with respect to how open government must be. Following the attack, the government launched a worldwide investigation into the terrorist group al-Qaeda and immediately took steps to protect the public from the scourge of terrorism. The intent was not to take away liberties but to provide protection.

Such was the purpose of the United States Congress in passing the Patriot Act, a behemoth law that seeks to give the government needed powers to combat the scourge of terrorism.

Supporters contend the Patriot Act is responsible for preventing further catastrophes. Senator Mitch McConnell (R-Kentucky), in a speech made in Congress in April 2004, noted that "the biggest hero to emerge from the hearings before the 9-11 Commission has been the Patriot Act."

As part of its terrorism investigation, the government detained more than 1,000 people. Some of the individuals faced deportation after it was discovered they had violated immigration laws. Some faced criminal charges; others were released. Information about these individuals had to be cloaked in secrecy to prevent other terrorists from escaping detention and creating further danger to the country and the world.

Freedom of information is a positive function in American society, but in the age of terrorism and modern communications, would-be terrorists can take advantage of our open society. Sometimes liberty must give way to basic order and survival.

Most Courts Have Recognized that the FOIA and First Amendment Rights Apply Differently in a Post-9/11 World

Admittedly, the United States Supreme Court has ruled that certain information must be open to the public. For example, in 1980, the U.S. Supreme Court ruled in *Richmond Newspapers, Inc.* v. *Virginia* that criminal trials generally must be open to the public.[2] The Court determined that experience and logic dictated that the trials should be open.

The experience prong asks whether there has been a history of openness to the information sought. In the *Richmond Newspapers* case, the Court noted that trials had been open to the public in Anglo-American history. The logic prong asks whether public access plays a positive role in the functioning of a particular governmental action. For instance, in *Richmond Newspapers*, the Supreme Court noted that open trials would further the process of truthfinding by exposing bias and partiality in the judicial process.

The U.S. Supreme Court has, however, developed other lines of cases that deal with access to government information in areas not traditionally open to the public. For example, the high court has ruled that the press has no First Amendment right of access to prisons.[3] Similarly, the high court has ruled that there is no First Amendment right that permits open access to addresses of persons arrested.[4] In that decision, the Court reasoned that "California could decide not to give out arrestee information at all without violating the First Amendment" because all the case in question involved was "nothing more than a governmental denial of access to information in its possession."

The access-to-prisons and access-to-arrestee-addresses cases provide the proper framework for courts to determine whether the media or other persons can obtain government information about material that pertains to the War on Terror. Neither the Freedom of Information Act nor the First Amendment requires the government to give out information that could benefit terrorists.

Public disclosure does not always advance the public interest. Sometimes, the public's interest is better advanced by giving government the opportunity to keep certain information confidential, particularly when confidentiality serves to provide protection. This rationale reflects the thinking in a post-9/11 world and the law enforcement exception to FOIA in general. Fortunately, many federal courts have realized that the post-9/11 world requires a reevaluation of both FOIA and the First Amendment.

There Is No Right to Obtain the Names of Post-9/11 Detainees

On October 29, 2001, the Center for National Security Studies filed a Freedom of Information Act request for the release of information about the detainees rounded up after September 11. The requested information included the names of the detainees, the names of their attorneys, the dates of arrest and release, the locations of their arrests and detention, and the reasons for detention.

The Department of Justice denied the FOIA request, relying on exemptions in the Freedom of Information Law. Specifically, the government relied on an exemption for law enforcement records.

THE LETTER OF THE LAW

5 U.S.C. 552(b)(7)

This section does not apply to matters that are ... (7) records or information compiled for law enforcement purposes, but only to the extent that the production of such law enforcement records or information

(A) could reasonably be expected to interfere with enforcement proceedings,

(B) would deprive a person of a right to a fair trial or an impartial adjudication,

(C) could reasonably be expected to constitute an unwarranted invasion of personal privacy,

(D) could reasonably be expected to disclose the identity of a confidential source, including a State, local, or foreign agency or authority or any private institution which furnished information on a confidential basis, and, in the case of a record or information compiled by criminal law enforcement authority in the course of a criminal investigation or by an agency conducting a lawful national security intelligence investigation, information furnished by a confidential source,

(E) would disclose techniques and procedures for law enforcement investigations or prosecutions, or would disclose guidelines for law enforcement investigations or prosecutions if such disclosure could reasonably be expected to risk circumvention of the law, or

(F) could reasonably be expected to endanger the life or physical safety of any individual.

After the government refused to release the information, the Center for National Security Studies filed suit in federal court to compel release of the information under FOIA. The Center for National Security also argued that the First Amendment required the government to release the documents. In August 2002, a federal district court ordered the government to disclose the names of the detainees and their attorneys. The district court, however, reasoned that the other information requested—the dates of arrest, location of the detainees and the reason for detainment—could be withheld under Exemptions 7(A) and 7(F).[5]

On appeal, the U.S. Circuit Court of Appeals for the District of Columbia ruled that the government did not even have to reveal the names of the detainees and their attorneys. The appeals court determined that Exemption 7(A) of FOIA applied, meaning that the release of the names could thwart enforcement proceedings.[6]

The appeals court reasoned that the government was entitled to deference in the context of FOIA claims when national security interests are present. The appeals court said the government was reasonable in fearing that the release of such names could give al-Qaeda vital information in regards to future terrorist attacks.

The appeals court reasoned that "a potential witness or informant may be much less likely to come forward and co-operate with the investigation if he believes his name will be made public."[7] The appeals court also rejected the plaintiffs' arguments that the detainee information must be disclosed under the First Amendment. The plaintiffs argued that the U.S. Supreme Court decision in *Richmond Newspapers, Inc.* v. *Virginia*—which held that criminal trials generally must be conducted in the open—also applied to the detainees' information. The appeals court disagreed, finding that the right of access recognized in *Richmond Newspapers* "does not extend to non-judicial documents that are not part of a criminal trial, such as the investigatory documents at issue here."[8] In rendering its decision, the court wrote, "We will not convert the First Amendment right of access to criminal judicial proceedings into a requirement that the government disclose information compiled during the exercise of a quintessential executive power—the investigation and prevention of terrorism."[9]

FROM THE BENCH

Center for National Security Studies **v.** *U.S. Department of Justice*, 331 F.3d 918 (D.D.C. 2003)

A complete list of names informing terrorists of every suspect detained by the government at any point during the September 11 investigation would give terrorist organizations a composite picture of the government investigation, and since these organizations would generally know the activities and locations of its members on or about September 11, disclosure would inform terrorists of both the substantive and geographic focus of the investigation. Moreover, disclosure would inform terrorists which of their members were compromised by the investigation, and which were not. This information could allow terrorists to better evade the ongoing investigation and more easily formulate or revise counter-efforts. In short, the records could reveal much about the focus and scope of the [agency's] investigation, and are thus precisely the sort of information exemption 7(A) allows an agency to keep secret.

While the name of any individual detainee may appear innocuous or trivial, it could be of great use to al-Qaeda in plotting future terrorist attacks or intimidating witnesses in the present investigations. . . . It is more than reasonable to expect that disclosing the name of every individual detained in the post-September 11 terrorism investigation would interfere with that investigation.

Similarly, the government's judgment that disclosure would deter or hinder cooperation by detainees is reasonable. The government reasonably predicts that if terrorists learn one of their members has been detained, they would attempt to deter any further cooperation by that member through intimidation, physical coercion, or by cutting off all contact with the detainee. A terrorist organization may even seek to hunt down detainees (or their families) who are not members of the organization, but who the terrorists know may have valuable information about the organization.

The Center for National Security Studies then appealed to the United States Supreme Court, but in January 2004, the Supreme Court declined to review the case.[10] Attorney General John Ashcroft applauded the Court's decision not to take the case:

> Time and time again, the courts have upheld the careful steps the Justice Department and federal government have taken since the devastating attacks of September 11, 2001 to both investigate that atrocity and prevent terrorists from striking again. We are pleased the court let stand a decision that clearly outlined the danger of giving terrorists a virtual roadmap to our investigation that could have allowed them to chart a potentially deadly detour around our efforts.[11]

• **How much deference do you think the government should receive when it says its motives are governed by national security interests?**

Special Interest Immigration Hearings Should Not Be Open to the Public

Many of the 9/11 terrorists came into the United States easily without being stopped by immigration and other government authorities. The U.S. government realized that immigration procedures needed to be tightened in order to root out some would-be terrorists. This does not mean, of course, that all immigrants should be viewed with suspicion. It does mean that immigration laws should be taken seriously and enforced. This is what happened immediately after 9/11.

Freedom of information disputes arose based on closed immigration hearings conducted by immigration judges. Especially in cases considered important and sensitive by the

Department of Justice—"special interest" cases—the government closed the hearings. Some freedom-of-information experts questioned the legality of these closed-door hearings. This dispute eventually led to a disagreement among the federal appeals courts over the closure of these special interest deportation hearings.

The better reasoned federal appeals court decisions revealed that national security concerns trump the public's right to know during the war on terrorism. Shortly after the 9/11 attack, Chief Immigration Judge Michael Creppy issued a memorandum implementing greater security measures surrounding deportation hearings. The memo required immigration judges to close "special interest" deportation hearings that dealt with aliens connected to terrorist activities or aliens that might possess information related to terrorist activities. The memo said that "the courtroom must be closed for these cases—no visitors, no family, and no press." The restrictions included "confirming or denying whether such a case is on the docket or scheduled for such a hearing."

Reporters for the *New Jersey Law Journal* and the *Herald News* challenged the constitutionality of the Creppy directive after they were denied information about these special interest deportation cases. They argued that the denial of access violated the First Amendment. The government countered that security required the closing of these hearings. A federal district court judge ruled in favor of the reporters, writing that there was a presumption of openness attached to deportation hearings. The district judge reasoned that these deportation hearings were similar to criminal trials, which the U.S. Supreme Court, in *Richmond Newspapers, Inc. v. Virginia,* had ruled were presumptively open. According to the district judge, there were "abundant similarities" between deportation hearings and criminal hearings.[12]

On appeal, a divided three-judge panel of the 3rd U.S. Circuit Court of Appeals reversed this ruling in *North Jersey*

Media Group, Inc. v. Ashcroft.[13] The appeals court majority reasoned that the government had many substantial security interests in this post-9/11 world.

The case arose in the wake of September 11, 2001, a day that changed American life drastically and dramatically. The era that dawned on September 11 and the war against terrorism that has pervaded the sinews of our national life since that day are reflected in thousands of ways in legislative and national policy, the habits of daily living, and our collective psyches. Because the primary national policy must be self-preservation, it seems elementary that, to the extent open deportation hearings might impair national security, that security is implicated in the logic test.

The court reasoned that "the tradition of open deportation hearings is too recent and inconsistent to support a First Amendment right of access."[14] Furthermore, the majority cited testimony from a counter-terrorism expert on how open deportation hearings might impair national security. This expert explained that information, that by itself might seem innocuous, can be combined with other information and provide key insights to terrorists. This "mosaic argument" has also been used in other cases.

The appeals court also reasoned that conducting open immigration hearings in these special interest cases could give would-be terrorist key insights into "the sources and methods of investigation." The appeals court also found persuasive five other reasons cited by the government's security expert in the case, Dale Watson, the FBI's Executive Assistant Director for Counterterrorism and Counterintelligence. These included the following points:

(1) Open hearings would allow the terrorists to see what types of "patterns of entry" were successful and unsuccessful;

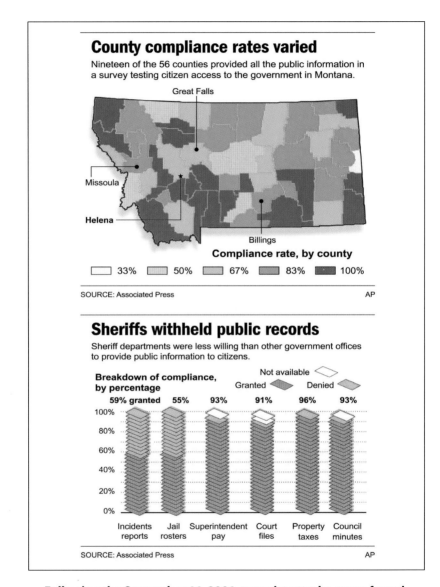

County compliance rates varied

Nineteen of the 56 counties provided all the public information in a survey testing citizen access to the government in Montana.

Compliance rate, by county

33%   50%   67%   83%   100%

SOURCE: Associated Press   AP

Sheriffs withheld public records

Sheriff departments were less willing than other government offices to provide public information to citizens.

Breakdown of compliance, by percentage

Not available   Granted   Denied

59% granted   55%   93%   91%   96%   93%

Incidents reports   Jail rosters   Superintendent pay   Court files   Property taxes   Council minutes

SOURCE: Associated Press   AP

Following the September 11, 2001, terrorist attacks, many feared that continuing to give the public complete access to certain information could cause security problems. Consequently, some states have changed their laws regarding public records or chosen not to abide by the existing laws. These charts show levels of compliance throughout the state of Montana in 2003.

(2) Open hearings would tell the terrorists what information the U.S. government lacks;

(3) Open hearings could give terrorists the knowledge necessary to speed up an attack if they realize the government is closing in on them;

(4) Open hearings that deal with evidence of terrorist links could give terrorists the chance to create false and misleading evidence or destroy existing evidence;

(5) Open hearings would destroy the privacy interests of the detainees.[15]

The court concluded by noting that the case must be considered "at a time when our nation is faced with threats of such profound and unknown dimension."[16]

Oftentimes, secrecy is absolutely vital. In this time of grave national security, leeway must be given to the government to operate secrecy. Open government works well in principle and, in theory, should be the governing rule, but the first job of government and law is to protect civilization and people from violence. Without freedom of violence, society cannot exist. That is why the government must be able to close deportation hearings or to conduct certain cases in secret. The M.K.B. case out of Florida, which is discussed in the next chapter, illustrates these points.

Summary
The Freedom of Information Act represents positive values, but sometimes ideals must give way to harsh realities. The reality is that we live in a changed world where dangerous terrorists can kill thousands if not millions of innocent people.

As one commentator has written, "The American public requires information, but too much information can cause security problems."[17] The Freedom of Information Act and the First Amendment are not a suicide pact. They should not be interpreted in a way that would hamper the pursuit of national security.

The Government Must Not Lose Its Democratic Nature in the Face of Terrorist Threats

We may be a lot closer to losing the war on terror than we realize. . . . The terrorists want us to live in fear, our leaders say. They want to change our way of life. They want to shake the underpinnings of our democracy. Well, they're succeeding. Sadly, however, this success results not from anything the terrorists have done but from our government's mistrust of its own people.

—Douglas Lee, First Amendment attorney[1]

In the war on terror, information is our most powerful weapon. But our leaders seem determined to disarm the American citizenry.

—Paul McMasters, First Amendment expert[2]

Since September 11, 2001, the U.S. government has aggressively pursued al-Qaeda and would-be terrorists. In the crackdown, the government has closed the channels of information.

A month after the terrorist strikes, Attorney General John Ashcroft issued a new policy directive to the heads of federal agencies with regard to the Freedom of Information Act. Ashcroft urged the agencies to carefully examine whether there were any possible ways to deny access to information within the existing exceptions to the law's supposed presumption of openness. In November, President George W. Bush signed an executive order restricting public access to the records of former presidents. Later that month, the president issued a military order saying that suspected terrorists could face charges before military tribunals with no public access. These actions have been termed "the sequence of secrecy." [3]

"Never in the nation's history has the flow of information from government to press and public been shut off so comprehensively and quickly as in the weeks following September 11," wrote Bruce Shapiro. According to Shapiro, "Much of the shutdown seems to have little to do with preventing future terrorism and everything to do with the Administration's laying down a new across-the-board standard for centralized control of the public's right to know." [4]

This information lockdown presents a problem in our constitutional democracy, which resides ultimate power in the people. In our society, the government must share power with the people. As First Amendment advocate Paul McMasters has said, "The primary means of sharing that power is the free and full flow of information from the government to the people and the people to the government." [5]

The 6th Circuit Properly Rejected the Blanket Ban on Access to Immigration Hearings

In the previous chapter, we learned that in *North Jersey Media Group, Inc.* v. *Ashcroft*, the 3rd U.S. Circuit Court of Appeals ruled that immigration hearings could be closed across the board to ensure national security. Another federal appeals court issued a very different opinion on the Creppy Memorandum.

Ten days after the horrific terrorist attacks of September 11, 2001, Chief Immigration Judge Michael Creppy issued a memorandum directing all immigration judges to close hearings involving so-called "special interest" deportation cases. The memorandum specified that government can classify certain deportation cases as "special interests" cases deserving of secrecy and closure. The Creppy Memorandum further required that all proceedings remain closed to the press, the public, and even the family members of a potential deportee.

In December 2002, an immigration judge in Michigan conducted a bond hearing for Rabih Haddad, a hearing that the government identified as a special interest case. Haddad, several newspapers, and Congressman John Conyers of Michigan challenged the closed deportation hearings for Haddad. The plaintiffs, including the newspaper the *Detroit Free Press*, contended that the Creppy directive violated the First Amendment. A federal district court sided with the plaintiffs, finding a First Amendment violation.[6]

On appeal, the U.S. Court of Appeals for the 6th Circuit agreed. In *Detroit Free Press* v. *Ashcroft*,[7] Judge Damon Keith, who wrote the court's majority opinion, determined that the deportation proceedings in the Haddad case should be open to the public generally. Judge Keith reasoned that the deportation hearings were similar to criminal trials, which the U.S. Supreme Court had declared open to the public in *Richmond Newspapers, Inc.* v. *Virginia*.[8] According to Judge Keith, "There are many similarities between judicial proceedings and deportation proceedings."[9]

Deportation hearings have traditionally been open to the public. In addition to this experience-based reasoning, Judge Keith noted that logic dictates that open deportation hearings serve the public interest. "Public access acts as a check on the actions of the Executive by assuring us that proceedings are conducted fairly and properly," he wrote.[10]

FROM THE BENCH

Detroit Free Press v. *Ashcroft,*
303 F.3d 681, 683 (6th Cir. 2002)

Today, the Executive Branch seeks to take this safeguard away from the public by placing its actions beyond public scrutiny. Against non-citizens, it seeks the power to secretly deport a class if it unilaterally calls them "special interest" cases. The Executive Branch seeks to uproot people's lives, outside the public eye, and behind a closed door. Democracies die behind closed doors. The First Amendment through a free press, protects the people's right to know that their government acts fairly, lawfully, and accurately in deportation proceedings. When government begins closing doors, it selectively controls information rightfully belonging to the people. Selective information is misinformation. The Framers of the First Amendment "did not trust any government to separate the true from the false for us." They protected the people against strict government.

Judge Keith articulated several, interrelated reasons why open deportation proceedings serve the public interest. These included:

- Public access serves as a check to make sure the proceedings are fair.

- Open hearings ensure that the government does not make mistakes.

- Open deportation hearings, particularly after September 11, 2001, "serve a 'therapeutic' purpose as outlets for 'community concern, hostility, and emotions.'"

- Open hearings give the perception of integrity and fairness.

- Public access gives individual citizens the ability to participate in our republican system of self-government.[11]

The 6th Circuit and Judge Keith agreed that the government had a compelling interest in combating terrorism. Nonetheless, the 6th Circuit determined that the government could combat terrorism by closing deportation hearings on a case-by-case basis rather than issuing a blanket, across-the-board ban. "Fittingly, in this case, the Government subsequently admitted that there was no information disclosed in any of Haddad's first three hearings that threatened 'national security for the safety of the American people,'" the court wrote.[12]

The government had argued that while a specific deportation hearing may present only a few bits of important information, that information could be part of a larger "mosaic" of how the government is fighting terrorism. Terrorist networks could piece together bits of information from different deportation hearings that could cause setbacks for the War on Terror.

The 6th Circuit said that perhaps there is some measure of truth to the "mosaic argument" but that it did not justify blanket closure. The court explained:

> Furthermore, there seems to be no limit to the Government's argument. The Government could use its 'mosaic intelligence' argument as a justification to close any public hearing completely and categorically, including criminal proceedings. The Government could operate in virtual secrecy in all matters dealing, even remotely, with "national security," resulting in a wholesale suspension of First Amendment rights. By the simple assertion of "national security," the Government seeks a process where it may, without review, designate certain classes of cases as "special

interest cases" and behind closed doors, adjudicate the merits of these cases to deprive non-citizens of their fundamental liberty interests.

This we simply may not countenance. A government operating in the shadow of secrecy stands in complete opposition to the society envisioned by the Framers of the Constitution.[13]

Judge Keith concluded that even in the face of tragedy, such as the atrocities committed on September 11, 2001, the nation must "be united in the wake of the destruction to demonstrate to the world that we are a country deeply committed to preserving the rights and freedoms guaranteed by our democracy."[14]

In *North Jersey Media Group, Inc.* v. *Ashcroft,* the 3rd U.S. Circuit Court of Appeals had reached the opposite conclusion, but the decision had not been unanimous.[15] Judge Anthony Scirica, now the Chief Judge of the 3rd Circuit, had disagreed with his colleagues on the majority opinion.

Although Judge Scirica recognized that the government had an exceedingly compelling interest in national security, he reasoned that the Creppy directive violated the First Amendment because it was a blanket ban on speech. According to Scirica, interests of national security could be addressed on an individualized basis rather than an across-the-board ban on speech.

"The stakes are high," the judge wrote. "Cherished traditions of openness have come up against the vital and compelling imperatives of national security. Because I believe national security interests can be fully accommodated on a case-by-case basis, I would affirm that part of the District Court's judgment."[16]

- **Which court do you think applied better reasoning in the immigration hearing cases?**

The Government Must Not Engage in a "Blackout of Justice" by Conducting Judicial Proceedings in Secret

Perhaps even more troubling than the closed immigration proceedings criticized so sharply by Judge Keith are the secret court cases occurring in the country without our knowledge. Secret court cases and closed dockets threaten, even destroy, the public's right to examine the judicial system.

In June 2004, the 2nd U.S. Circuit Court of Appeals ruled that the public has a qualified First Amendment right to inspect court docket sheets. The case arose after it was discovered that Connecticut's state court system had maintained a secret court system for certain cases, often involving wealthy litigants.

The court determined that both experience and logic weighed in favor of public access to court docket sheets. "History therefore demonstrates that docket sheets and their equivalents were, in general, expected to remain open for public viewing and copying," the court wrote.[17] The court further concluded that "docket sheets enjoy a presumption of openness and that the public and the media possess a qualified First Amendment right to inspect them."[18]

One commentator has referred to this dangerous development as a "blackout of justice."[19] The case of Mohamed K. Bellahouel provides an example of this. Bellahouel, an Algerian-born waiter detained by U.S. authorities shortly after the September 11 attacks, was imprisoned at a detention center in Miami for five months. Apparently, Bellahouel was considered a "material witness" because he had served two of the hijackers at a restaurant and had entered a movie theater with a third hijacker. While he was imprisoned, Bellahouel filed a writ of habeas corpus in federal court, challenging his confinement as unlawful.

The strange thing about his case was that it was not listed on the court's docket. In fact, the only reason anyone knows about this case is that a court clerk mistakenly entered it on a court listing of cases, designating it with the word "SEALED." Dan Christensen, a reporter with the *Miami Daily Business Review*, noticed the case was listed on the docket and then removed the next day.

Bellahouel filed an appeal all the way to the United States Supreme Court, arguing that the lower courts had violated the First Amendment and the principles of open government by handling his case in secrecy. According to Bellahouel's legal papers, the secret handling of the case violated the guarantee of public access to judicial proceedings.[20]

The Reporters Committee for Freedom of the Press and more than 20 other media organizations filed an amicus brief with the U.S. Supreme Court in *M.K.B.* v. *Warden.* "The excessive

Quotable: Douglas Lee

While no one disputes the notion that investigations and prosecutions of terrorists require some secrecy, that need cannot justify the creation of secret court dockets and blanket closure orders. Our judicial system has been rooted in a presumption of openness, a presumption that can be overcome only in limited circumstances and only after evidence is introduced demonstrating why closure is necessary. Even when secret court proceedings or hearings are allowed, the presumption of openness has required that the existence of the case and its non-secret aspects be open and available to the public. Bellahouel's case is a drastic departure from this tradition. It exemplifies a completely secret court system, one hidden from the news media and the American people. No one knows how many cases like Bellahouel's exist; for all we know, hundreds of detainees could be claiming mistreatment by the government. The government, of course, is happy to litigate these cases in secrecy. Why, after all, would it want to be accountable to its citizens for detentions that appear in many cases to be based on little more than racial profiling? The judiciary's willingness to participate in this secrecy, however, is deeply troubling.[22]

secrecy surrounding M.K.B.'s petition would be inexcusable under any circumstances, but it is particularly egregious in a case of potentially significant news value," the brief read. The attorneys for the plaintiff also noted that "Details of M.K.B.'s arrest and confinement could spark a healthy debate about the means by which the government is conducting the war on terrorism."[21] The U.S. Supreme Court denied the petition for review.

Summary

The United States must not forget why we are fighting the war on terrorism. We are fighting the war on terrorism to ensure that democratic rule prevails over tyranny and despotism. We must, however, not sacrifice our civil liberties in the War on Terror. As Benjamin Franklin once said, "Those who would give up essential liberty to purchase a little temporary safety deserve neither liberty nor safety."

U.S. Supreme Court Justice Sandra Day O'Connor said it best in the Court's June 2004 opinion in *Hamdi* v. *Rumsfeld*, a ruling on a matter that involved whether the detainees at Guantanamo Bay, Cuba, could challenge their detentions in U.S. courts. Justice O'Connor wrote:

> Striking the proper constitutional balance here is of great importance to the Nation during this period of ongoing combat. But it is equally vital that our calculus not give short shrift to the values that this country holds dear or to the privilege that is American citizenship. It is during our most challenging and uncertain moments that our Nation's commitment to due process is most severely tested; and it is in those times that we must preserve our commitment at home to the principles for which we fight abroad.[23]

The words of Justice O'Connor must be taken to heart during the war on terrorism. The country must not lose its commitment to freedom, democracy, and openness during times of struggle in a post-9/11 world.

The Military's Interest in National Security Trumps the Press's First Amendment Rights

In plain language, the news media today have no legal way to force their way onto the battlefield.

—Frank Aukofer and William Lawrence

The military's mission is to win battles and defeat opposing forces. The military's mission is not to inform the public or the press of its plans. The great Chinese warrior-writer Sun Tzu wrote in *The Art of War* that the "formation and procedure used by the military should not be divulged before-hand."[1] Obviously, if the military had to alert the press to its every move beforehand, military success and national security could be compromised. Military success often requires both security and surprise.

"Throughout history the U.S. government has not held its military operations open to the public," one commentator recently wrote, adding that "operational security and the element

54

of surprise are essential to conducting successful warfare and thus required a controlled press."[2] The press should be prevented from published crucial, important military "after-the-fact" information. As another commentator has written, "Secrecy remains important even after a mission has been accomplished."[3]

For this reason, the Department of Defense can impose the restrictions it considers necessary to ensure success on the battlefield. Sometimes media representatives complain about necessary arrangements such as pooling, or grouping, press representatives into certain groups or areas. For example, in 1983, the U.S. military conducted a successful, three-day invasion of the island of Grenada. President Ronald Reagan ordered military leaders to exclude the news media from the first two days of the attack. The experience outraged many in the press who believed they had a right to view the invasion firsthand.

Media representatives also complain about policies of security review. Security review refers to the military policy of reviewing media news copy before general release to ensure that no valuable or classified information is released that could help the enemy or otherwise compromise the military mission. Security review has been used effectively since World War II.[4] During the Desert Storm invasion of the Persian Gulf in 1991, the military again used the process of security review. This process helped the military to engage in another successful military mission, freeing Kuwait from the grips of Iraqi dictator Saddam Hussein.

In the opinion of the commentator cited above, "A reporter with unlimited access to American military plans and strategies poses a direct and serious threat to the safety of American forces if that reporter improvidently leaks such information. . . . The pooling arrangements provide a narrowly tailored check on such a threat."[5]

Security review is important in a military context. The same commentator further explained that "security review of material obtained by the press in time of war ensures that the enemy does not receive information it could use against American forces during war." [6]

First Amendment advocates may criticize security review, pooling arrangements, and other military decisions as censorship. These critics do not fully understand that First Amendment rights are not absolute and that sometimes even preemptive restraints on publication have been judged constitutional. As the United States Supreme Court stated in 1931, "No one would question but that a government might prevent actual obstruction to its recruiting service or the publication of the sailing dates of transports or the number and location of troops." [7]

History Reveals That the Media Has Never Had Unfettered Access to the Battlefield

It is a myth that the press has had a historical right of access to the battlefield. In fact, throughout America's history, the military has always placed limits upon media coverage. George Washington complained bitterly about news media coverage of the Revolutionary War. "It is much to be wished that our printers were more discreet in many of their publications," he said. "We see in almost every paper proclamations or accounts transmitted by the enemy of an injurious character." [8]

After defeating the British at the Battle of New Orleans during the War of 1812, General Andrew Jackson imprisoned a news editor who would not agree to Jackson's demands to consult him before printing material about the war. [9] During the Civil War, the government had to restrain the press from reporting about sensitive war information. In April 1861, the federal government under President Abraham Lincoln took control of telegraph lines to and from Washington, D.C. General William Tecumseh Sherman blamed the press for the defeat of the Union Army at the first Battle of Bull Run. He blamed the *Washington Star* and *The New York Times* for listing the order of battle. [10]

In March 1862, Secretary of State Edwin Stanton ordered the seizure of the offices of *The Sunday Chronicle*, which had published information on military matters. During the Spanish-American war, the military banned the media from entering combat zones.[11] In World War I, Congress passed the Espionage Act, prohibiting publication of material that could aid the enemy. President Woodrow Wilson created the Committee on Public Information, which sought to control press coverage of the war. The committee revoked reporters' press passes if they failed to have their stories checked by censors.

During World War II, Congress passed the War Powers Act, which led to the creation of the Office of War Information and the Office of Censorship. These agencies implemented press codes that instructed journalists on what information they could print. Military censors curbed the release of information or news that was deemed harmful to the military missions. General Douglas MacArthur routinely censored the press, ordering stories pulled if he did not like them.[12]

During the Korean War, reporters were prohibited from writing stories about food shortages, inferior U.S. equipment, and corruption in the South Korean government. Stories were not allowed if they would "cause embarrassment to the United States or its allies."[13]

The Vietnam War witnessed numerous reporters covering the war and criticizing the war effort. Many reporters noted the "credibility gap" between military claims of progress and what they saw with their own eyes. The war led to greater distrust between the military and the media.[14]

The Courts Recognize That the Press Does Not Have a First Amendment Right to the Battlefield

The courts have uniformly rejected publishers' efforts to assert First Amendment right of access claims to the military battlefield. In several cases, the courts have ruled that the press' claims were moot or no longer active. For example, in 1983 Larry Flynt, the publisher of *Hustler* magazine, argued that the exclusion of the press from Grenada during the first two days of the invasion was a constitutional violation. Flynt asked a federal judge to prohibit the Department of Defense from hindering news-gathering efforts.

A federal judge dismissed the action as moot, saying it was no longer a live, legal controversy. The judge did this in part because the three-day invasion was already completed.[15] Additionally, some reporters had been allowed to cover the conflict during the third and final day of the invasion. Similarly, a federal judge rejected a First Amendment challenge filed by *The Nation* over censorship of the press during the Persian Gulf conflict.[16]

Flynt, the publisher of *Hustler*, later sued Secretary of Defense Donald Rumsfeld, claiming that the Department of Defense had violated his First Amendment rights by delaying his access to the battlefields in Afghanistan. He had faxed a letter to government officials, asking that correspondents for his magazine be permitted free access to "U.S. military operations in Afghanistan and other countries where hostilities may be occurring as part of Operation Enduring Freedom." Not satisfied with the reply he received, Flynt filed suit in federal court on November 16, 2001. The district court rejected his First Amendment arguments.[17]

On appeal, the U.S. Court of Appeals for the District of Columbia also rejected Flynt's constitutional claims, writing, "There is nothing we have found in the Constitution, American history, or our case law to support this claim."[18] Flynt had argued that the courts should find for right of access for the press to the military, based on the U.S. Supreme Court's decision in *Richmond Newspapers, Inc. v. Virginia*. In *Richmond Newspapers*, the U.S. Supreme Court applied the "logic and experience" test to determine that both reasoning and history support a right of access of the press to attend criminal trials.[19]

The government responded that the proper analogy was not to the Court's decision in *Richmond Newspapers* but to its 1978 decision rendered in *Houchins* v. *KQED*, a case which involved press access to prisons. In *Houchins*, the U.S. Supreme Court ruled that the press had no general right of access to prisons and that the First Amendment does not "mandate a right of access to government information or sources of information within the government's control."[20]

"As an initial matter, the history of press access to military units is not remotely as extensive as public access to criminal trials," the appeals court wrote in rejecting Flynt's claim. "No comparable history exists to support a right of media access to U.S. military units in combat."[21] The appeals court also pointed out that Flynt and his correspondents were eventually granted access to parts of the battlefield.

> - **Should there be a difference in terms of public access between a criminal trial and a military battlefield?**

The decision comports with an earlier decision by the U.S. Court of Appeals for the District of Columbia, holding that the press did not have a right of access to the return of caskets of deceased soldiers from overseas to military bases in the United States. The military prevented journalists' and photojournalists' access to the military dead to protect the privacy rights of the deceased soldiers' family members.

FROM THE BENCH

Flynt v. *Rumsfeld*, 355 F.3d 697 (D.C. Cir. 2004)

The facial challenge is premised on the assertion that there is a First Amendment right for legitimate press representatives to travel with the military, and to be accommodated and otherwise facilitated by the military in their reporting efforts during combat, subject only to reasonable security and safety restrictions. There is nothing we have found in the Constitution, American history, or our case law to support this claim.

To support the position that there is such a constitutional right, appellants first point to cases that discuss the general purposes underlying the First Amendment. ...These cases, however, say nothing about media access to the U.S. combat units engaged in battle.

The appeals court upheld the military policy, stating, "It is obvious that military bases do not share the tradition of openness on which the Court relied in striking down restrictions on access to criminal court proceedings in *Press Enterprise, Richmond Newspapers,* and *Globe Newspapers.*"[22]

Summary
The media's First Amendment rights must take a backseat to military necessities and national security values. The press is an important institution that can serve as a useful check on the three official branches of government. Because the ultimate interest of a country is survival, military information should be released only if it is abundantly clear that it will not adversely

FROM THE BENCH

JB Pictures, Inc. v. Department of Defense, 86 F.3d 236 (D.C. Cir. 1996)

The government also asserts an interest in protecting the privacy of families and friends of the dead, who may not want media coverage of the unloading of caskets at Dover. The strength of the interest will of course vary with the pattern of use of Dover: the smaller the number arriving at any given time, and the smaller the number of occasions of arrival, the easier it is for outsiders to infer the identify of the individual soldier. In any event we do not think the government hypersensitive in thinking that the bereaved may be upset at public display of the caskets of their loved ones. We note that the government's policy of allowing the family the right to deny access to services at the home base is consistent with its assertion of this interest behind the policy at Dover. Accordingly, we have no hesitation in concluding that there was nothing impermissible about the access restrictions imposed at Dover Air Force Base.

Because the access policy at Dover does not violate the First Amendment's guarantees of freedom of speech and of the press, and because the complaint does not embrace a claim based on the right to engage in on-base speech, the judgment of the district court is AFFIRMED.

affect military personnel, the military mission, and the morale of the troops.

Given the incredible state of technological advances, the need for media self-restraint and military control is even greater. As one legal commentator has written, "At no time have restrictions been more crucial than now due to the ability of the press to disseminate information globally and the concomitant ability of anyone to receive it." [23]

The government went out its way during the Iraqi war to provide the media access to the war effort. In fact, the government embedded many journalists with troop divisions. These media representatives have been able to provide first-hand, up-close and personal accounts of the harrowing experiences of war. They have also shown the brutality of war.

It is critical to understand, however, that before there can be liberty, there must be order. As previously noted, the first job of a government and a legal system is to protect civilization from violence. The military is the entity that protects civilization. Freedom of the speech and press are important values in a constitutional democracy, but let us not make any mistake about it. Freedom of speech and press must not interfere with military secrets and national security.

Quotable: Attorney Carlos Kelly

Journalistic zeal, ordinarily a desired quality of the press, in time of war can be a flaw, which can have far-reaching, and dire, consequences. During the Gulf War, some journalists disclosed sensitive information; other journalists unnecessarily put U.S. forces in harm's way when their overzealous pursuit of a story led to their capture by Iraqi forces. Given these incidents from a previous conflict, and the attitudes of some journalists in the aftermath of September 11, the need for a sensible media policy based upon the media's exercise of self-restraint becomes clear.

Source: Carlos A. Kelly, "The Pen is Mightier Than the Sword, or Why the Media Should Exercise Self-Restraint in Time of War," 77 Fla. B.J. 22 (Jan. 2003).

The Press and the Public Deserve Information About Military Matters

Secrecy in government is fundamentally anti-democratic, perpetuating bureaucratic errors. Open debate and discussion of public issues are vital to our national health. On public questions, there should be uninhibited, robust and wide-open debate.

—Supreme Court Justice William O. Douglas

Those who saw the attack upon Baghdad, Iraq, in March 2003 will never forget the sight. The U.S. military bombarded the city and stronghold of dictator Saddam Hussein with a campaign known as "Shock and Awe." For the first time in history, the American public witnessed the live invasion of a foreign city with their own eyes on their own television screens.

The reason that the average citizen could watch the Shock and Awe military campaign was that journalists were "embedded" with American troops. The policy sought to give the press greater access to military activities. Victoria Clarke, assistant secretary of defense for public affairs, commented on the embedding of journalists: "So far, the embedding seems to have gone very well. Americans and people around the world are seeing firsthand the wonderful dedication and discipline of the coalition forces."[1]

Embedded journalists represented a victory of sorts for the media. In 1995, authors Frank Aukofer, a journalist, and William Lawrence, a retired Navy admiral, wrote: "The only realistic way for the news media to cover modern warfare is for reporters to be positioned in and travel with military units, preferably as soon as the action starts."[2] Aukofer and Lawrence's wish for embedded reporters became a reality in the war on Iraq.

This was a major improvement for the media who were excluded from military campaigns on the island of Grenada in 1983 and in the Persian Gulf in 1991. During these conflicts, many journalists felt that they had been denied important channels of information and could not serve as an effective conduit for the public.

The press is often called the fourth estate because of its important role in informing the public about the three branches of the government—the executive, the legislative, and the judicial. The press serves as the eyes and ears of the public and a check upon the government. If the government denies access to the press, then the press cannot perform these valuable functions. Former U.S. Supreme Court Justice William O. Douglas once wrote, "The dominant purpose of the First Amendment was to prohibit the widespread practice of governmental suppression of embarrassing information."[3]

Freedom of the press also gives members of the media the right to report on embarrassing military information, such as the abuse of Iraqi prisoners at Abu Ghraib by U.S. military personnel. The scandal, reported by journalists such as Seymour Hersch for *The New Yorker*, shocked much of the world. Such reports, however, demonstrate the meaning of "freedom of the press." No matter how one feels about the war in Iraq or other military missions, the public has a right to know about the country's military operations. Without a free press, the public's right to know will be severely curtailed.

The public deserves to know about war and military matters because these are sometimes the most important events in history. On occasion, the press has been able to exercise its right to report in these events. For example, the Associated Press, perhaps the most respected press organization in the world, was created during the Civil War to provide press reports. When government operates in shrouds of secrecy, the public is denied the opportunity to participate in the open constitutional democracy known as the United States of America.

The First Amendment Must Not Be Sacrificed on the Altar of National Security

The First Amendment is our blueprint for personal freedom and the hallmark of a democratic government. It provides that the governed retain the ultimate power. Obviously, First Amendment rights are not absolute. Justice Oliver Wendell Holmes recognized that the First Amendment does not protect someone who falsely shouts "fire" in a theater. Similarly, national security interests can trump free-press concerns but only where it has been clearly shown that the publication of certain material would infringe on national security.

In *New York Times Co.* v. *United States*, the U.S. Supreme Court ruled in 1971 that the government could not prohibit two newspapers, *The New York Times* and *The Washington Post*, from publishing a classified study entitled "History of U.S. Decision-Making Process on Vietnam Policy." The study, which consisted of more than 7,000 pages, called into question U.S. policy with regard to Vietnam since the 1950s. The study also increased public opposition to the war.

The government sought an emergency injunction to prohibit further publication of the study in the newspapers. The U.S. Supreme Court rejected the government's position in a 6–3 vote.

Nearly all of the justices wrote separate opinions. First Amendment absolutist Justice Hugo Black, who looked upon any restriction upon freedom of speech or of the press with strong cynicism and distrust, rejected the government's position that publishing the Pentagon Papers would threaten national security.

Justice William O. Douglas agreed, noting in his separate opinion, "The dominant purpose of the First Amendment was to prohibit the widespread practice of governmental suppression of embarrassing information."[4] Justice William Brennan also wrote an opinion highly protective of First Amendment values. He considered the government's national security argument but said that such a defense should be interpreted quite narrowly.

FROM THE BENCH

Justice Hugo Black's opinion in *New York Times Co.* v. *U.S.* (1971)

In the First Amendment the Founding Fathers gave the free press the protection it must have to fulfill its essential role in our democracy. The press was to serve the governed, not the governors. The Government's power to censor the press was abolished so that the press would remain forever free to censure the Government. The press was protected so that it could bare the secrets of government and inform the people. Only a free and unrestrained press can effectively expose deception in government. And paramount among the responsibilities of a free press is the duty to prevent any part of the government from deceiving the people and sending them off to distant lands to die of foreign fevers and foreign shot and shell. In my view, far from deserving condemnation for their courageous reporting, *The New York Times*, *The Washington Post*, and other newspapers should be commended for serving the purpose that the Founding Fathers saw so clearly. In revealing the workings of government that led to the Vietnam War, the newspapers nobly did precisely that which the Founders hoped and trusted they would do.

The word "security" is a broad, vague generality whose contours should not be invoked to abrogate the fundamental law embodied in the First Amendment. The guarding of military and diplomatic secrets at the expense of informed representative government provides no real security for our Republic.

Brennan wrote, "Thus, only governmental allegation, and proof that publication must inevitably, directly, and immediately cause the occurrence of an event kindred to imperiling the safety of a transport already at sea can support even the issuance of an interim restraining order."[5]

While the Pentagon Papers case involves prior restraint of a publication and does not involve access to the military battlefield, some view the results as an important directive on how the military must treat the media. Law professor Mark C. Rahdert has suggested that decisions made in the Pentagon Papers case "at least lend some force to the notion that governmental power to censor during wartime is subject to fairly strict limits and that any permissible censorship must be supported by specific national security needs."[6]

Security Review Represents Censorship at Its Core and a Violation of the First Amendment

In the nomenclature of the military, security review represents the censorship of journalists covering military matters. The military reviews journalists' material before publication to ensure that the material does not compromise national security or other important governmental interests. Many commentators criticize security review as pure censorship. For instance, Frank Aukofer and William Lawrence wrote: "Censorship—or security review, as it is called in military language—is a phenomenon of the past."[7]

The press does not constitute a threat to national security. As lawyer-journalist C. Robert Zelnick wrote:

> The press rarely poses any kind of danger to national security. The goal of defense officials, military or civilian, who seek to keep the press on a short leash is, in most instances, to control the editorial slant of what is reported rather than to protect tactical, strategic, or national security from the unauthorized disclosure of sensitive material.[8]

Quotable: Professor William Lee

First Amendment rights are fragile. Conversely, the incentives for government officials to misuse mechanisms such as 'security review' are powerful. Given this imbalance, "security review" of news stories from the battlefield should be avoided. Instead, the military should protect security by exercising care over what it discloses to the press. In addition, prior to allowing the press to observe military operations, the military should brief the press as to the types of information that, if published, would harm operational security. Once the ground rules are explained, the press should be left alone.

Source: William E. Lee, "Security Review and the First Amendment," 25 Harv. J.L. & Pub. Pol'y 743 (2002).

Critics will argue that the Pentagon Papers case dealt with publication rather than initial access or newsgathering. This view ignores the fact that newsgathering and publication go hand-in-hand. Without newsgathering in the first place, there can be no publication. As the U.S. Supreme Court stated in 1972, "Nor is it suggested that news gathering does not qualify for First Amendment protection; without some protection for seeking out the news, freedom of the press could be eviscerated."[9]

- **Should newsgathering receive as much First Amendment protection as publication?**

The Press Should Have a Qualified Right of Access to Military Combat Missions

The courts have not been very friendly to media claims of a right of access to the battlefield. This is unfortunate because throughout much of America's history, the media has enjoyed a right of access to military matters. Commentator Michael D. Steger wrote:

The first two hundred years of the use of American military force saw the media enjoy broad access to theaters of operation. Only in certain instances in the Civil War and the Spanish-American War were American reporters excluded from the front lines. In World War I, World War II, and the Korean War, the press received wide access to most aspects of combat. Likewise, in Vietnam, the media enjoyed unparalleled access to virtually every aspect of the conflict.[10]

Steger also observed that the Supreme Court has recognized a qualified right of the press to enter criminal trials and prisons. In his opinion, the Court should apply the same reasoning to military combat zones:

A right of press access to combat operations can be analogized from the right of press access to prisons and criminal trials. While the Supreme Court has stated that the right to gather information and news does not exist in all contexts and is not absolute, it is nevertheless an implied right. This right is only one of access to combat operations and does not include an affirmative duty on the part of the government to provide the press with information. When media coverage of large-scale military operations is viewed in light of both the press' role as the substitute for the American public and the historical function of the press in covering the American military, a media right of access to combat situations can be seen.[11]

The Supreme Court recognized, in *Richmond Newspapers, Inc.* v. *Virginia,* that criminal trials should be open to the public, noting the history of open criminal trials. Two years later in *Globe Newspaper Co.* v. *Superior Court,* the Supreme Court struck down a Massachusetts statute that required the automatic closure of courts hearing rape cases. Justice William Brennan wrote, "Where the State attempts to deny the right of access in order to inhibit the disclosure of sensitive information, it must be shown that the denial is necessitated by a compelling governmental interest and is narrowly tailored to serve that interest."

The Supreme Court's ruling in these cases suggests right of access to military zones should be available (1) if there is a history of openness of military areas to the press or (2) if the right of access serves the military process in general. These two prongs are sometimes called the "logic and experience" test. If these two criteria are met, media access can be restricted only if the military can show that the denial of access serves a compelling governmental interest and is narrowly drawn to serve that compelling interest.[12]

The First Amendment also recognizes the right of the public to receive information and ideas. This means that the public has an independent right, apart from the right of the press, to acquire information about the war. "The potential of this well settled right to receive information as a basis for claims of access to combat activities and defense operations, remains to be tested in the military setting," wrote law professor Robert O'Neil. "Yet, it has much potential, especially in tandem with claims reflecting the historic openness of battlefields and other sectors."[13]

Summary

The public has a right to know about what occurs in wars, especially when Americans are dying on the battlefield and in foreign lands. National security, of course, is a compelling interest of the highest order. Too often, however, the term "national security" is used as an excuse to deny information the government would prefer to keep secret. As Justice Hugo Black warned, "The guarding of military and diplomatic secrets at the expense of informed representative government provides no real security for our Republic."

Cameras Distort Trial Proceedings and Should Be Prohibited

I think the case is so strong that I can tell you that the day you see a camera come into our courtroom it's going to roll over my dead body.

—U.S. Supreme Court Justice David Souter
in 1996 to a Senate subcommittee[1]

Trial by television is, therefore, foreign to our system. . . . The television camera is a powerful weapon. Intentionally, or inadvertently, it can destroy an accused and his case in the eyes of the public.

—U.S. Supreme Court Justice Tom Clark in *Estes* v. *Texas*, 1965

In July 1954, Marilyn Sheppard was brutally murdered in a suburb of Cleveland, Ohio. Authorities charged her husband Dr. Sam Sheppard with murder. The sensational nature of the case attracted enormous publicity, led to multiple trials, and eventually inspired the hit television series *The Fugitive* and a movie by the same title.

One of the problems with Sheppard's first trial, which ended in a guilty verdict, was the presence of television reporters and newspaper photographers in the courtroom. Consider the following passage from the U.S. Supreme Court, which describes the chaotic nature of the courtroom proceedings:

> The courtroom remained crowded to capacity with representatives of news media. Their movement in and out of the courtroom often caused so much confusion that, despite the loudspeaker system installed in the courtroom, it was difficult for the witnesses and counsel to be heard. Furthermore, the reporters clustered within the bar of the small courtroom made confidential talk among Sheppard and his counsel almost impossible during the proceedings. They frequently had to leave the courtroom to obtain privacy. And many times when counsel wished to raise a point with the judge out of the hearing of the jury it was necessary to move to the judge's chambers. Even then, news media representatives so packed the judge's anteroom that counsel could hardly return from the chambers to the courtroom.[2]

This is what can happen with cameras in the courts. The news media can dominate a courtroom and deprive a criminal defendant of a fair trial. In 1966, the U.S. Supreme Court determined that Dr. Sam Sheppard had been denied his right to a fair trial in part because of the disruptive conduct of the press. Although technological improvements have helped lessen to some extent the intrusiveness of the media, there is no denying that sometimes cameras wield a negative influence.

High-profile trials are not a new phenomenon. The criminal trial of former football great O.J. Simpson comes to mind as a recent example, but there were other trials that also captivated the public and initiated a media onslaught. For instance, in 1935, Bruno Hauptmann was charged with the kidnapping and murder of famous aviator Charles Lindbergh's baby son. The Hauptmann trial was referred to as a "Roman holiday" because photographers overwhelmed the courtroom, engaging in intrusive behavior. "Roman holiday" refers to a loud, raucous, party-type atmosphere—certainly not the type of atmosphere necessary to conduct a trial. In the Hauptmann trial, photographers interfered with the attorneys' tables and shoved their cameras into witnesses' faces. Needless, to say the trial was disrupted and those concerned with the judicial system were far from pleased. In fact, the conduct at the Hauptmann trial led the American Bar Association to adopt a canon in 1937 that prohibited the taking of photographs during court proceedings.

American Bar Association Canon 35 (1937)

Proceedings in court should be conducted with fitting dignity and decorum. The taking of photographs in the courtroom, during sessions of the court or recesses between sessions, and the broadcasting of court proceedings, degrade the court and create misconceptions with respect thereto in the mind of the public and should not be permitted.

- **Do you think cameras in court lead to less dignity and decorum?**
- **Do you think that the media can conduct themselves in a way that would allow camera coverage of courtroom proceedings?**

Television Cameras Are a Distorting, Disruptive Influence

Television cameras in the courtroom distort trial proceedings, threaten the fair-trial rights of criminal defendants and create undue pressure upon trial participants. The First Amendment does provide the public right of access to most criminal and civil trials. This right of access, however, allows actual physical presence in the courtroom not a visual gateway to millions of people.

Camera Coverage Is Not Constitutionally Required. In Fact, the Sixth Amendment May Disallow It

The right of access to a courtroom is not absolute. The First Amendment is not the only constitutional gem in the crown of the Bill of Rights. Other amendments carry equal weight and must be considered before judicial decisions are made. The Sixth Amendment guarantees that criminal defendants are entitled to a fair trial. The U.S. Supreme Court has declared that in the context of a trial, the defendant's fair trial rights are paramount. This means that a judge must give greater concern to whether a criminal defendant receives a fair trial than to whether the public's desire for information is satisfied.

In handing down its decision in *Estes* v. *Texas*, the U.S. Supreme Court wrote: "We have always held that the atmosphere essential to the preservation of a fair trial—the most fundamental of all freedoms—must be maintained at all costs."[3] The Supreme Court in the *Estes* case reversed a criminal defendant's swindling conviction because the televising of his court proceedings created a sensational atmosphere that deprived him of his fundamental right to a fair trial. The Court noted the negative impact that televised proceedings would have on jurors, witnesses, trial judges, and the defendant.

- **How should the court balance a free press with a fair trial?**
- **Which constitutional right should predominate?**

With respect to witnesses, the Court explained: "The quality of the testimony in criminal trials will often be impaired. The impact upon a witness of the knowledge that he is being viewed by a vast audience is simply incalculable."[4] The Court also noted that supervising televised trials would place a heavy burden upon trial judges, making their task "much more difficult and exacting."[5]

FROM THE BENCH

Estes v. *Texas*, 381 U.S. 532 (1965)

The potential impact of television on the jurors is perhaps of greatest significance. They are the nerve center of the fact-finding process. It is true that in most States like Texas where they are required to be sequestered in trials of this nature the jurors will probably not see any of the proceedings as televised from the courtroom. But the inquiry cannot end there. From the moment the trial judge announces that a case will be televised it becomes a cause celebre. The whole community, including prospective jurors, becomes interested in all the morbid details surrounding it. The approaching trial immediately assumes an important status in the public press and the accused is highly publicized along with the offense with which he is charged. Every juror carries with him into the jury box these solemn facts and thus increases the charge of prejudice that is present in every criminal case. And we must remember that realistically it is only the most notorious trial which will be broadcast, because of the necessity for paid sponsorship. The conscious or unconscious effect that this may have on the juror's judgment cannot be evaluated, but experience indicates that it is not only possible but highly probable that it will have a direct bearing on his vote as to guilt or innocence. Where pretrial publicity of all kinds has created intense public feeling which is aggravated by the telecasting or picturing of the trial the televised jurors cannot help but feel the pressures of knowing that friends and neighbors have their eyes on them.

Moreover, while it is practically impossible to assess the effect of television on jury attentiveness, those of us who know juries realize the problem of jury 'distraction.' The State argues that is *de minimis* since the physical disturbances have been eliminated. But we know that distractions are not caused solely by the physical presence of the camera and its telltale red lights. It is the awareness of the fact of televising that is felt by the juror throughout the trial. We are all self-conscious and uneasy when being televised. Human nature being what it is, not only will a juror's eyes be fixed on the camera, but also his mind will be preoccupied with the telecasting rather than with the testimony.

The Court saved its harshest criticism for how the camera would affect criminal defendants. The camera "is a form of mental—if not physical—harassment, resembling a police line-up or the third degree," the Court wrote. "A defendant on trial for a specific crime is entitled to his day in court, not in a stadium, or a city or nationwide arena. The heightened public clamor resulting from radio and television coverage will inevitably result in prejudice. Trial by television is, therefore, foreign to our system. Furthermore, telecasting may also deprive an accused of effective counsel."[6]

The Court continued: "The television camera is a powerful weapon. Intentionally or inadvertently it can destroy an accused and his case in the eyes of the public."[7] Fifteen years later, the U.S. Supreme Court again addressed the issue of cameras in the courtroom. In *Chandler* v. *Florida*, the Court ruled that the presence of cameras in a courtroom did not amount to an automatic denial of a criminal defendant's due process rights. Nonetheless, the Court cautioned that trial judges must take precautions to ensure that cameras do not disrupt trial proceedings. Chief Justice Warren Burger wrote that "the risk of prejudice to particular defendants is ever present and must be examined carefully as cases arise."[8] What this means is that courts must still closely scrutinize the presence of cameras in courtrooms to determine whether they will have a disruptive influence on trials.

> • **Was the Supreme Court right in calling television cameras a "form of mental—if not physical—harassment"?**

Law professor Christo Lassiter has cited several reasons why cameras should be barred from courtrooms, arguing that cameras would cause trial participants to feel undue pressure and act differently than they would without cameras. "Given the concerns about the media ability to distort, which is greatly magnified by television, the proper balance is struck under both the First and Sixth Amendment guarantees by allowing the print media in the courtroom, but drawing the line at still and moving picture cameras," Lassiter wrote.[9]

The Federal Rules of Criminal Procedure Still Ban Cameras

The federal rules of criminal procedure still prohibit cameras in federal criminal trials. Federal Rule of Criminal Procedure, Rule 53 provides: "The taking of photographs in the court room during the progress of judicial proceedings or radio broadcasting of judicial proceedings from the courtroom shall not be permitted by the court."

In *United States* v. *Moussaoui*, a federal district court decided that Rule 53 is constitutional. *Court TV* and other media entities argued that the public had an interest in seeing the trial proceedings of Moussaoui, who was accused of being a member of the al-Qaeda conspiracy that attacked the World Trade Center in Manhattan and government buildings in Washington, D.C.

The press argued that the First Amendment guarantees the public the right of access to criminal trials. Members of the media contended that this right of access included a right to televised proceedings. The court disagreed, reasoning that right of access was satisfied by allowing members of the general public and the press to be present at the trial proceedings.

The press also argued that the federal ban on courtroom cameras discriminated against the electronic media in favor of the print media. The court rejected this argument, reasoning that the electronic media could attend the trial physically the same as members of the print media. "As a 'reasonable manner' restriction on access to public proceedings, Rule 53 limits only the equipment members of the media are permitted to bring into the courtroom."[10]

The court further explained: "Nothing in Rule 53 prevents members of electronic media from attending the trial, taking notes while seated in the gallery and reporting about it. Members of the print media are similarly deprived of the tools of their trade, including lab top computers, cell phones, hand-held organizers and other electronic devices."[11]

U.S. v. *Moussaoui,* 205 F.R.D. 183 (E.D. Va. 2002)

The public's right of access is constitutionally satisfied when some members of both the public and the media are able to attend the trial and report what they have observed. . . . These constitutional requirements are fully met by the way the Moussaoui proceedings are being conducted. An audio-visual feed of the proceedings to a nearby courtroom has increased seating capacity to 200 seats, about one half of which are reserved for the media and the other half for the general public. Daily transcripts will be electronically available within three hours of the close of each day's court session as was done in *United States* v. *McVeigh*, No. 96-CR-68-M (W.D. Okl.). These arrangements fully satisfy the constitutional requirements for openness and accessibility. Moreover, the immediate availability of the transcripts will avoid the concerns expressed by the intervenors about minimizing inaccurate reporting.

The court also ruled that even if Rule 53 were unconstitutional, it would still deny access in this particular case. The presiding judge determined that broadcasting this trial "is likely to intimidate witnesses and jurors, as well as threaten the security of the courtroom and all those involved in this trial." [12] The safety of trial participants would be severely compromised, the judge reasoned, by allowing their faces to be shown to the public. Terrorists, including potential terrorist cells in the United States, could use that information to cause harm to the trial participants.

Many States Provide Only Limited Camera Coverage of Courtroom Proceedings

Although nearly all states allow some form of camera coverage, the right is far from absolute. In fact, some states allow camera coverage only in certain courts. For example, the State of New York allows camera coverage only in its appellate courts. A state civil rights law prohibits camera coverage in New York trial courts.

Then New York Governor Thomas E. Dewey signed this measure into law in 1952. He stated: "It is basic to our concept of justice that a witness compelled to testify have a fair opportunity to present his testimony. No right is more fundamental to our traditional liberties. The use of television, motion pictures and radio at such proceedings impairs this basic right." [13]

Recently, a New York trial court upheld the constitutionality of Civil Rights Law Section 52 from a constitutional challenge brought by *Court TV*. *Court TV* argued that an experimental period allowing some courtroom camera coverage in the state should be permanently extended and the old rule discarded as unconstitutional. *Court TV* argued that the 1952 law should not bar cameras in the twenty-first century when cameras are no longer operated in an intrusive fashion. The court recognized that *Court TV* had a point: "There is no dispute that *Court TV*'s small, silent, remote-controlled camera utilizing only natural light, does not present the physical problems of television coverage which beset a bygone era." [14] The court noted, however, that there was evidence that the behavior of witnesses, judges, and jurors had been altered by courtroom coverage.

THE LETTER OF THE LAW

New York Civil Rights Law § 52

No person, firm, association, or corporation shall televise, broadcast, take motion pictures or broadcast or arrange for the televising, broadcasting or taking of motion pictures within this state of proceedings, in which the testimony of witnesses by subpoena or other compulsory process is or may be taken, conducted by a court, commission, committee, administrative agency or other tribunal of this state.

Other states have also restricted coverage. For example, Alabama allows coverage in criminal cases only if the prosecutor and the defendant and their attorneys give written consent. Similarly, in civil cases in Alabama, all litigants and their attorneys must give written consent. In Arkansas, a judge can authorize camera coverage in a trial but any objection by a party or a party's attorney will end such coverage. Many states provide camera access only to appellate courts. The concern is that cameras will negatively impact jurors and others at the trial court level.

- **Does your state restrict camera coverage in courts?**

FROM THE BENCH

Courtroom Television Network LLC v. State of New York, 769 N.Y.S.2d 70, 87-88 (2003)

More important, the vast record developed during New York's ten-year experiment contains ample evidence from which the Legislature could rationally conclude that Civil Rights Law § 52 advances the State's interest in fair trials. As the New York experience developed, and observation of the experiments became successfully more objective and comprehensive, concerns about the effect of audio-visual coverage on trial participants persisted and even increased. There was credible testimony that some witnesses had been deterred from testifying by the prospect of being filmed, while others had been negatively affected at trial. There was testimony that audio-visual coverage had meaningfully affected judges' behavior at a core level—by changing how they issued orders. There was evidence that jurors' behavior could significantly be altered by cameras. There was the testimony of scholars who, after careful study of the issue, concluded that televised trials present fundamental challenges to fairness by allowing external social pressures to exert influence in the courtroom. And, there was resounding evidence that the public, after years of exposure to cameras, remained skeptical of their value, were less inclined to testify in front of cameras, and had developed an aversion to having their own trials covered.

Quotable: Thomas Sowell (2002)

Putting cameras in the courtrooms is one of those ideas that sounds good—until you see how televising congressional hearings has led to politicians hamming it up for the folks back home, instead of doing the work in a sober, timely and thoughtful way.

Source: Thomas Sowell, "Random Thoughts," Townhall.com, 4/26/02. Available online at: *http://www.townhall.com/columnists/thomassowell/ts20020426.shtml.*

As mentioned earlier, cameras in the courtroom become an even greater problem in high-profile criminal cases. In the *People* v. *Orenthal James Simpson*, cameras helped turn a criminal case into a worldwide—and at times sensational—public spectacle. Gerald F. Uelman, one of Simpson's defense attorneys and a law school dean, wrote about the cameras in the case: "Our courtrooms are among the last refuges for rational discourse in a world drowning in hype. Once we convert the courtroom to a 'set,' we transform the lawyers, witnesses, and judges into 'performers.'"[15] This phenomenon caused Uelman to argue that cameras should be barred from certain, very high-profile criminal trials. "For a 'trial of the century,' adding television cameras in the courtroom is like throwing gasoline on a fire. It transforms the proceedings into a sort of 'hype heaven,' where exaggeration knows no limits," he observed.[16]

Summary

Cameras in the courtroom, if properly utilized, can enhance public understanding of the judicial system. Cameras also affect the conduct of trial participants—attorneys, parties, witnesses, jurors, and even judges. This fact calls into question whether cameras can ensure the constitutionally guaranteed right of a fair trial. Even former U.S. Supreme Chief Justice Warren Burger, who ruled in favor of opening criminal trials to the press, balked when the issue came to cameras in the United States Supreme Court.

There is no constitutional right to have a camera in a courtroom. The First Amendment guarantees only that criminal trials generally remain open. It does not guarantee that cameras must be permitted. A television reporter can attend a trial just like any other citizen. Cameras should be permitted only if all sides consent to their usage and only if the judge takes extra precautions to ensure the safety of all trial participants.

Cameras in the Courtroom Enhance Public Knowledge of and Give Greater Credibility to Our Judicial System

People in an open society do not demand infallibility from their institutions, but it is difficult for them to accept what they are prohibited from observing.

—Chief Justice Warren Burger[1]

The O. J. Simpson criminal case generated a great deal of criticism and resulted in many proposals to eliminate or at least limit camera access to court proceedings. Ironically, the case actually helped create a better understanding of the criminal justice system. Many professors used the case as an ideal teaching tool for their law school classes or introduction to criminology undergraduate courses. Georgetown law professor Paul F. Rothstein, who has taught a class entitled "Evidence: The O. J. Case," commented in *The National Law Journal*, "It's good pedagogy to suck the students in for the right or wrong reasons, and then teach them something." The professor also noted: "If it's illustrated in a living, breathing way, it's understood better rather than cases from a casebook."[2]

Thus, even the case some see as the worst example of courtroom camera access has actually had a positive educational impact. Courtroom cameras also give the public crucial insight into the workings of the judicial branch of government, something seen far more rarely than the workings of the executive and legislative branches of government. The president gives press conferences and speaks to the nation during state of the union and other addresses. Congress holds much business before public view, particularly with the advent of C-SPAN. On the other hand, the public at large gets to see far less of the work of the judicial branch, particularly in the federal courts. Many high-profile trials are not televised. The public must rely on the reports of journalists in the courtroom.

Cameras provide the public with knowledge about the functioning of the criminal justice system, educate students from grade school to law school about trials, and advance First Amendment interests. The First Amendment generally prohibits government officials from operating in shrouds of secrecy and keeping its citizens in the dark. Cameras would further the First Amendment purpose of providing a free flow of information to the public.

The First Amendment provides that information about public institutions should flow to the public. Cameras further this interest by letting the public see what happens inside the courtroom.

The Trend in the United States Is Toward Greater Acceptance of Courtroom Camera Coverage

The trend is moving toward greater acceptance of electronic coverage of courts. An Oklahoma judge first allowed cameras into an American courtroom in December 1953. In January 1956, the Colorado Supreme Court conducted the first hearings on cameras in courts and determined that cameras should not be banned but that the individual judge should have discretion.[3]

Currently, all 50 states allow some level of electronic coverage in some courts. Only the District of Columbia prohibits trial and appellate coverage entirely. Many states allow television courtroom cameras by leaving the decision to the discretion of individual trial judges. Other states allow coverage of appellate cases while prohibiting coverage of trial cases. Appellate cases are cases that have been appealed to a higher court. Whereas trial courts involve witnesses, jurors, and a single judge, appellate court proceedings normally occur with attorneys on both sides arguing to a panel of judges.[4]

Cameras Do Not Distort Trial Proceedings

The case against cameras in the courtroom intensified after the highly publicized 1995 "trial of the century" in which a California jury acquitted former football great Orenthal James (O. J.) Simpson of the murder of his ex-wife Nicole Brown Simpson and her companion, Ronald Goldman. Judge Lance Ito allowed cameras in the courtroom, and the nation, as well as the jury and courtroom spectators, saw attorneys Johnnie Cochran, Marcia Clark, Christopher Darden, and others argue the case.

Many private citizens and legal commentators who disagreed with the verdict blamed cameras in part for the outcome, but cameras simply gave the public a window into an often mysterious judicial system. They helped rather than harmed the legal system. The O. J. Simpson criminal case—no matter how one feels about the jury's verdict—raised public consciousness on numerous important issues, including spousal abuse, police perjury, racism and perceived racism in the criminal justice system, the general racial

THE LETTER OF THE LAW

Rule 2.170, Florida Rules of Judicial Administration

(a) Electronic and Still Photographic Coverage Allowed. Subject at all times to the authority of the presiding judge to: (1) control the conduct of proceedings before the court; (2) ensure decorum and prevent distractions; and (3) ensure the fair administration of justice in the pending cause, electronic media and still photography coverage of public judicial proceedings in the appellate and trial courts of this state shall be allowed in accordance with the following standards of conduct and technology promulgated by the Supreme Court of Florida.

(b) Equipment and Personnel

(1) At least 1 portable television camera, operated by not more than 1 camera person, shall be permitted in any trial or appellate proceeding. The number of permitted cameras shall be within the sound discretion and authority of the presiding judge.

(2) Not more than 1 still photographer, using not more than 2 still cameras, shall be permitted in any proceeding in a trial or appellate court.

(3) Not more than 1 audio system for radio broadcast purposes shall be permitted in any proceeding in a trial or appellate court. Audio pickup for all media purposes shall be accomplished from existing audio systems present in the court facility. If no technically suitable audio system exists in the court facility, microphones and related wiring essential for media purposes shall be unobtrusive and shall be located in places designated in advance of any proceeding by the chief judge of the judicial circuit or district in which the court facility is located.

(4) Any 'pooling' arrangements among the media required by these limitations on equipment and personnel shall be the sole responsibility of the media without calling upon the presiding judge to mediate any dispute as to the appropriate media representative or equipment authorized to cover a particular proceeding. In the absence of advance media agreement on disputed equipment or personnel issues, the presiding judge shall exclude all contesting media personnel from a proceeding.[5]

divide, the jury system, evidence law, and media fairness or lack thereof.

> • **Did watching a case on *Court TV* or another station increase your knowledge of the legal system?**

There Should Not Be a "Media Circus" Exception to Camera Coverage

Government officials should not bar cameras simply because an occasional case may turn into a media circus. There have always been media circuses, whether cameras were present or not. The 1807 treason trial of former Vice President Aaron Burr, the 1925 Scopes "monkey" trial in Dayton, Tennessee, and the Bruno Hauptmann trial of 1935 are prime examples. These cases were the "trials of the century" of their time. They were media circuses even without television cameras in the courtroom. Here it is important to ask which trial educated the public more:

Quotable: Steven Brill, Founder of *Court TV*

Let's be blunt. The reason that the issue of cameras in the courtroom is again under debate in the legal community is because the Simpson case, to many Americans, has made the legal system look bad. And so some lawyers and judges are afraid that the public will want to change the system. And some judges even resent the idea that the public is so closely watching one of their colleagues at work and having the temerity to criticize how they are performing their jobs.

First, to the extent that televising the Simpson case has made the public question various aspects of the legal system, that is an argument for cameras, not against them. Isn't that exactly what is supposed to happen in a democracy? The press shines light on a governmental activity so that the public can evaluate it. It is as if we suddenly moved to ban reporting about wars simply because the coverage of the Vietnam War caused lots of people to question it.

Source: From Steven Brill, "That's Entertainment! The Continuing Debate Over Cameras in the Courtroom," *Federal Lawyer* (July 1995).

the O. J. Simpson criminal trial with a camera present or the O. J. Simpson civil trial that was closed to cameras?

Unfortunately, as commentator Fred Graham noted after the O. J. Simpson trials, "judges are carving out a 'high profile' exception to the laws allowing cameras in court."[6] Graham has explained the faulty reasoning for this high-profile exception to cameras in the courtroom:

> The most frequent reason given is that televising high-interest cases may upset witnesses or jurors. But there's no evidence that anybody who would be unnerved by a camera wouldn't be equally unstrung by the intensity of a major case with the courtroom crammed with print reporters and the cameras waiting outside. In fact, no coherent rationale has been given for creating a 'high-profile' exemption, and cameras are allowed in routine cases as fully as ever.[7]

Cameras often cover attorneys and others on the court-house steps. Rules of court strictly limit what an attorney may say in court during a trial. The rules do not generally provide nearly the same level of constraint on the courthouse steps. Camera coverage on the courthouse steps often creates the real media circus, if there is one, more so than cameras at the actual trial. "The television camera assures greater accuracy, less bias, and more direct observation of the trial," wrote author and Simpson appellate attorney Alan Dershowitz. Elaborating on this point, Dershowitz added:

> But most of the real costs erroneously attributed to the televising of trials are more correctly attributable to the trying of cases in the media. The television camera is far more disturbing on the courthouse steps than it is in the court-room itself. Nearly everything bad that the camera can do in the courtroom can be made worse on the courthouse steps.[8]

Quotable: Alan Dershowitz

It makes little sense, in my view, to censor the only unbiased, direct, and entirely truthful reporter of the trial—the courtroom television camera—while still allowing extensive coverage by more biased, partisan, and inaccurate human reporters. Our Constitution would not permit us to adopt the British system, which is tantamount to censorship; nor would its adoption be wise as a matter of policy. Watergate, Whitewater, and many other scandals would never have been exposed under the English rules.

Source: Alan Dershowitz, *Reasonable Doubts*. New York: Simon & Schuster, 1996.

- **Do you agree with Alan Dershowitz that cameras do not inject bias into cases?**

A concern with cameras in courts has been their affect on jurors and whether jurors will be intimidated by the presence of cameras. According to famed attorney Johnnie Cochran, cameras make jurors believe that the case has a "heightened level of importance."[9] This fact causes jurors to take their civic responsibility more seriously and issue better verdicts.

Cameras Do Not Threaten the Fair-trial Rights of Criminal Defendants

Some criminal defense attorneys also argue that television cameras threaten a criminal defendant's right to a fair and impartial jury under the Sixth Amendment of the Constitution. The Sixth Amendment, in essence, provides for a fair trial. Attorney Cochran has disputed the notion that cameras threaten a defendant's fair-trial rights: "I think that cameras would ensure their client's getting a fair trial," he has said. "From the defense standpoint, I find that it's helpful to me. Every time I've had a camera, I've won."[10]

Even the U.S. Supreme Court has recognized that cameras do not per se violate the constitutional rights of the accused.

The U.S. Supreme Court has not explicitly ruled that the First Amendment requires cameras in the courts, but in the 1980 case *Richmond Newspapers, Inc.* v. *Virginia,* the Court did rule that criminal trials must be open to the public.[11] The Court also ruled, in the 1981 decision on *Chandler* v. *Florida,* that the State of Florida had not violated the fair-trial rights of four defendants because their trial proceedings were televised.[12]

The case involved four former Miami Beach policemen who were tried for conspiracy to commit burglary, grand larceny, and other crimes after allegedly breaking into a well-known restaurant. The defendants were convicted in a televised trial. On appeal, the defendants contended that the presence of cameras in their trial was an automatic denial of due process. The Court rejected that argument, writing:

> An absolute constitutional ban on broadcast coverage of trials cannot be justified simply because there is a danger, that in some cases, prejudicial broadcast accounts of pretrial and trial events may impair the ability of jurors to decide the issue of guilt or innocence uninfluenced by extraneous matter. The risk of juror prejudice in some cases does not justify an absolute ban on news coverage of trials by the printed media; so also the risk of such prejudice does not warrant an absolute constitutional ban on all broadcast coverage.[13]

Chandler v. *Florida* stands for the principle that cameras do not per se violate the Sixth Amendment rights of criminal defendants. After the Chandler decision, many other states began experimenting with cameras.

Future of Cameras

Cameras appear to be here to stay in the state court system. The federal courts tell a much different story. In 1996, the federal

Judicial Conference allowed the experimental use of cameras in some federal courtrooms. After three years, the Judicial Conference decided not to continue the experiment.

For several years, Rep. Steve Chabot (R-OH) and Senator Charles Schumer (D-NY) have introduced measures in the U.S. House of Representatives and the U.S. Senate respectively to allow cameras in the federal courts. The congressmen first introduced the "Sunshine in the Courtroom Act" in 1997. The measure does not force cameras on federal judges. Instead, it gives both federal trial and appellate courts the option of allowing cameras.

In 2000, such a measure passed the House but never made it out of the Senate. The Senate Judiciary Committee passed a similar camera in federal courts bill, but the full Senate never voted on the measure. Chabot and Schumer introduced similar bills in 2003.

H.R. 2155 (2003)

In the twenty-first century, the people of the United States obtain information regarding judicial matters involving the Constitution, civil rights, and other important legal subjects principally through the print and electronic media. Television, in particular, provides a degree of public access to courtroom proceedings that more closely approximates the ideal of actual physical presence than newspaper coverage or still photography.

Providing statutory authority for the courts of the United States to exercise their discretion in permitting televised coverage of courtroom proceedings would enhance significantly the access of the people to the Federal judiciary.

Notwithstanding any other provision of law, any presiding judge of a district court of the United States may, in his or her discretion, permit the photographing, electronic recording, broadcasting, or televising to the public of court proceedings over which that judge presides.

> • **Do you think Rep. Chabot's proposal to give federal judges the option to allow cameras in federal courts is a good idea?**

———————•————————•————————•————————

Summary

Americans need to know about their judicial system. The average citizen does not have the time to enter a courtroom and personally observe how the system works. For this reason, the camera enables the average citizen to view government in action. Not allowing camera coverage deprives individual citizens of their rights to learn more about the justice system.

In 2003, the 9th U.S. Circuit Court of Appeals allowed camera coverage of the California recall election hearing. The hearing was shown on C-SPAN and contributed to greater public knowledge about an important public event. Even the O.J. Simpson trial, for all its notoriety, helped the public learn more about the criminal justice system and various societal issues of great importance. Federal appeals court Judge Richard Arnold said it best:

> My general feeling is that the public owns the courtroom. They pay for it, it's part of their government. And the more they know about what goes on there, the better, in the long run, the courts will be. Because the public can, if it thinks that things are going wrong, form a view and express that view, and the judges can try to do better.[14]

The Future of Open Government

The United States of America prides itself on freedom, openness, democracy and popular rule. The country prides itself on information, what First Amendment expert Paul McMasters terms "the currency of the realm in a democratic republic." Even though the Founding Fathers operated in complete secrecy when they created the Constitution in the summer of 1787, they established a government that has developed a tradition of openness.

This tradition consists of the first 45 words of its Bill of Rights, known as the First Amendment, which protects individuals' freedom of speech and freedom of the press. Federal and state laws provide that the government generally must operate in the sunshine and avoid secrecy. The federal Freedom of Information Act is the prime example of a law designed to force government to operate in the open. But, even this law has had a rough history. In 1996, McMasters said that "much of the first 30 years of the Freedom of Information Act has been a struggle to survive." There have been highs and lows in FOIA and the public's right to know. On the one hand, Congress amended the FOIA to apply to electronic communications with a law sometimes called EFOIA. The law amended FOIA to apply its requirements to the electronic format. On the other hand, the U.S. Supreme Court has recognized broad privacy interests in determining whether exemptions in the FOIA apply to prevent the release of information to the public.

Suffice it to say that sometimes other values conflict with freedom of information. The debates over cameras in the court, press access to the military, privacy exemptions in the FOIA and national security interests in the post-9/11 world show a tension between openness and other interests. Denying camera coverage of the courts arguably denies the public important information about the judicial system. On the other hand, the Constitution requires that criminal defendants receive a fair trial by an impartial jury. The conflict between these competing interests shows that there are often not any easy answers.

Even more important in today's world is the need for open government when there is the compelling need to ensure security. The age-old balance between liberty and security sometimes requires that we sacrifice some liberty in order to have greater security. Hopefully, government leaders will calibrate that balance by respecting the hallowed principle of open government.

The Founding Fathers never knew a threat like Osama Bin Laden and probably never envisioned terrorists flying airplanes crashing into skyscrapers killing thousands of innocent people. After September 11, the world and the culture in America changed. National security has become a preeminent value.

Similarly, the technological advances in the age of the Internet have caused even greater fear about invasions of privacy. People's personally identifiable information is transmitted easily, leading to cases of identify theft, embarrassment and other problems. Society has shown an increased sensitivity to privacy concerns, what Justice Louis Brandeis referred to in 1890 as "the right to be let alone." That notion of privacy even found its way in the federal Freedom of Information Act as discussed in an earlier chapter.

The tradition of open government conflicts with an urgent need for greater national security and an increasing development of privacy law. It is unlikely that the United States of America will lose all of its commitment to open government. Hopefully, it will not lead, in the words of James Madison, to a "Farce or a Tragedy."

However, many view the current environment as one damaging to freedom of information and the public's right to know. In the age of terrorism and the greater protection of privacy, the struggle to protect the public's right to know continues and intensifies. In September 2004, a federal judge in New York ordered the Department of Defense to release documents on the treatment and detentions of prisoners in U.S. custody at Abu Ghraib prison in Iraq. U.S. District Judge Alvin K. Hellerstein wrote: "Ours is a government of laws, laws duly promulgated and laws duly observed. No one is above the law; not the executive, not the Congress, and not the judiciary. One of our laws is the Freedom of Information Act (FOIA). That law, no less than any other, must be duly observed." The judge accused the government of operating at a "glacial pace" with respect to producing requested documents regarding the treatment of prisoners.

This legal skirmish will not be the last over government information relating to the war effort, security in a 9/11 world and government policy in the War on Iraq. Security sometimes demands that the channels of communication be temporarily closed. But, as Benjamin Franklin said years ago: "They who would give up an essential liberty for temporary security, deserve neither liberty or security."

Introduction

1 Al Knight, *The Life of the Law.* New York: Crown Publishers, 1996, p. 4.

2 Quoted in Paul McMasters, "Homeland Security FOIA Exemption Leaves Us in the Dark," First Amendment Center Online, 5/10/03. Available online at *http://www.firstamendmentcenter.org/ commentary.aspx?id=11460.*

3 S. 609 (2003).

4 Josh Meyer, "Reporters Battle for Information in War on Terrorism," *The News Media & the Law* (Fall 2002), p. 11.

5 Jeff Lemberg, "Pleading the First: The Public's First Amendment Right of Access to High-profile Trials Is at Risk, as More and More Judges Shield Court Proceedings From the News Media," *News Media & The Law* (Spring 2004), p. 7–10.

Point: Privacy Rights Often Must Trump the Free Flow of Information

1 Louis Brandeis and Samuel D. Warren, The Right to Privacy, 4 Harv L. Rev., 1983 (1890).

2 Statement of President Lyndon Johnson, 7/4/66. Available online at *http://www.gwu.edu/~nsarchiv/nsa/ foia/FOIARelease66.pdf.*

3 5 U.S.C. § 552 (b)(6).

4 5 U.S.C. § 552(b)(7)(C).

5 510 U.S. 487 (1994).

6 Ibid., 500–501.

7 124 S.Ct. 1570 (2004).

8 124 S.Ct. at 1577.

9 Ibid. at 1578.

10 Ibid. at 1579.

11 Ibid. at 1580–81.

12 Ibid. at 1582.

13 489 U.S. 749 (1989).

14 Ibid., 770.

15 821 So.2d 388 (Fla. App. 5th Dist. 2002).

16 Ibid., 402.

17 Hoefges, et al., p. 5.

18 Keith Anderson, "Is There Still a Sound Legal Basis: The Freedom of Information Act in the Post 9/11 World," 64 Ohio St. L.J. 1605 (2003).

Counterpoint: Freedom of Information Is a Paramount Value Serving a Powerful Public Interest

1 Burt A. Braverman and Frances J. Chetwynd, *Information Law: Freedom of Information Privacy Open Meetings Other Access Laws,* New York: Practicing Law Institute, 1985, Section 1–1.1.

2 Ibid., Section 1–1.2.

3 Statement of President Lyndon Johnson, 7/4/66. Available online at *http://www.gwu .edu/~nsarchiv/nsa/foia/FOIARelease66.pdf.*

4 Ibid.

5 *Department of the Air Force* v. *Rose*, 425 U.S. 352 (1976).

6 5 U.S.C. § 552(a)(3)(A).

7 David C. Vladeck, "Freedom of Information Overview," First Amendment Center Online. Available online at *http://www.firstamendmentcenter.org/ press/information/overview.aspx.*

8 Memorandum of Attorney General John Ashcroft to Heads of All Federal Departments and Agencies, 10/12/01. Available online at *http://www.usdoj .gov/foiapost/2001foiapost19.htm.*

9 Ibid.

10 Quoted in Jennifer LaFleur, "Privacy Tops Reasons Agencies Withhold Information," *The News Media & the Law,* (Summer 2003). Available online at *http://www.rcfp .org/news/mag/27-3/foi-privacy.html.*

11 *Department of Air Force* v. *Rose*, 425 U.S. 352, 38 (1976).

12 Ken Paulson, "Supreme Court Places a Premium on Privacy," First Amendment Center Online, April 1, 2004. Available online at *http://www.firstamendment-center.org/commentary.aspx?id=13104.*

13 Tony Mauro, "Supreme Court's ruling marks blow to public's right to know," *USA Today,* April 6, 2004. Available online at *http://www.usatoday.com/ news/opinion/editorials/2004-04-06-scotus-edit_x.htm.*

14 Ibid.

15 Rebecca Daugherty, "Dead Weight in the Balance," *The News Media & the Law* (Spring 2004), p. 35.

16 Favish at 1577.

17 Amicus Brief of the Reporters Committee for Freedom of the Press et al. in *Office of Independent Counsel* v. *Favish* (02-954), p. 16–17.

Point: Public Information Concerns Must Give Way to Security in a Post-9/11 World

1 *Center for National Security Studies* v. *U.S. Department of Justice*, 331 F.3d 918, 935 (2003).

2 *Richmond Newspapers, Inc.* v. *Virginia*, 448 U.S. 555 (1980).

3 *Houchins* v. *KQED*, 438 U.S. 1 (1978).

4 *LAPD* v. *United Reporting Publ'g Corp.*, 528 U.S. 32 (1999).

5 *Center for National Security Studies* v. *U.S. Department of Justice*, 215 F.Supp.2d 94 (D.D.C. 2002).

6 *Center for National Security Studies* v. *U.S. Department of Justice*, 331 F.3d 918 (3rd Cir. 2003).

7 Ibid., p. 345.

8 Ibid., p. 349.

9 Ibid., p. 350.

10 *Center for National Security Studies* v. *United States Department of Justice* (03–472).

11 Bill Mears, "Supreme Court Rejects Appeal Over Secret 9/11 Detentions," CNN.com, 1/12/04. Available online at *http://www.cnn.com/2004/LAW/01/12/scotus.terrorism.secrecy/*.

12 *North Jersey Media Group, Inc.* v. *Ashcroft*, 205 F.Supp.2d 288, 300 (D.N.J. 2002).

13 308 F.3d 198 (3rd Cir. 2002).

14 Ibid., 211.

15 Ibid., 218.

16 Ibid., 220.

17 "Disclosure of Government Information Online: A New Approach From an Existing Framework," 15 Harv. J. Law & Tech. 497, 514–515 (2002).

Counterpoint: The Government Must Not Lose Its Democratic Nature in the Face of Terrorist Threats

1 Douglas Lee, "Official secrecy helps terrorists undermine democracy," First Amendment Center Online, 1/13/04.

Available online at *http://www.firstamendmentcenter.org/commentary.aspx?id=12454*.

2 Paul K. McMasters, "Over-reaching secrecy undermines America's safety," First Amendment Center Online, 6/20/04. Available online at *http://www.firstamendmentcenter.org/commentary.aspx?id=13538*.

3 Travis Loop, "Stepping Up Secrecy: The Delicate Balance of Press Freedom and National Security in the Post-Sept. 11 World," *Presstime*, September 2003, p. 36.

4 Bruce Shapiro, "Information Lockdown," AlterNet, 10/29/01. Available online at *http://www.alternet.org/module/printversion/11816*.

5 Paul McMasters, "Denial of Access Shushes the Democratic Dialogue," First Amendment Center Online, 12/12/01. Available online at *http://www.freedomforum.org/templates/document.asp?documentID=15517*.

6 *Detroit Free Press* v. *Ashcroft*, 195 F.Supp.2d 937 (E.D. Mich. 2002).

7 303 F.3d 681 (6th Cir. 2002).

8 448 U.S. 555 (1980).

9 303 F.3d at 699.

10 Ibid. at 703.

11 Ibid. at 703–705.

12 Ibid. at 709.

13 Ibid. at 709–710.

14 Ibid. at 711.

15 308 F.3d 198 (3rd Cir. 2002).

16 Ibid., 228 (J. Scirica, dissenting).

17 *The Hartford Courant* v. *Pellegrino*, 371 F.3d 49 (2nd Cir.)(6/8/04).

18 Ibid., p. *36.

19 James McClaughlin, "Blackout of Justice," Reporters Committee for Freedom of the Press (Winter 2004). Available online at *http://www.rcfp.org/mag/28-1/cov-blackout.html*.

20 Ibid.

21 Amicus Brief of the Reporters Committee for Freedom of the Press, *M.K.B.* v. *Warden* (03–6747).

22 Douglas Lee, "Official Secrecy Helps Terrorists Undermine Democracy," First Amendment Center Online, 1/13/04. Available online at *http:// www.firstamendmentcenter.org/ commentary.aspx?id=12454.*

23 *Hamdi* v. *Rumsfeld* (03-6696).

Point: The Military's Interest in National Security Trumps the Press's First Amendment Rights

1 Carlos A. Kelly, "The Pen is Mightier Than the Sword or Why the Media Should Exercise Self-restraint in Time of War," 77 Fla. B.J. 22, 24 (Jan. 2003).

2 Brian William DelVecchio, "Press Access to American Military Operations and the First Amendment: The Constitutionality of Imposing Restrictions," 31 Tulsa L.J. 227, 247 (1995).

3 Kelly, p. 24.

4 Frank Aukofer and William Lawrence, "America's Team: The Odd Couple, Freedom Forum, 1995, p. 25. Available online at *http://www.firstamendment-center.org/PDF/americasteam.PDF.*

5 Ibid. 249.

6 Ibid., 250.

7 *Near* v. *Minnesota*, 283 U.S. 697, 717 (1931).

8 Aukofer and Lawrence, p. 35.

9 Ibid.

10 Ibid., p. 36.

11 Ibid., p. 37.

12 Ibid., p. 38.

13 Ibid., p. 39.

14 C. Robert Zelnick, "The Press and National Security: Military Secrets and First Amendment Values," 1 J. Nat'l Security L. 21, 30 (1997).

15 *Flynt* v. *Weinberger*, 588 F.Supp. 57 (D.D.C. 1984).

16 *Nation Magazine* v. *Department of Defense*, 762 F.Supp. 1558 (S.D.N.Y. 1991).

17 *Flynt* v. *Rumsfeld*, 180 F.Supp.2d 174 (D.D.C. 2002).

18 *Flynt* v. *Rumsfeld*, 355 F.3d 697, 703 (D.D.C. Cir. 2004).

19 448 U.S. 555 (1980).

20 438 U.S. 1, 15 (1978).

21 Flynt, 355 F.3d at 704.

22 *JB Pictures, Inc.* v. *Department of Defense*, 86 F.3d 236, 240 (D.C. Cir. 1996).

23 DelVecchio, p. 250.

Counterpoint: The Press and the Public Deserve Information About Military Matters

1 Quoted in Jim Garamone, "Press and Military Seem to Appreciate Media Embeds," American Armed Press Service, 3/26/03. Available online at *http://www.dod.mil/cgi-bin/dlprint .cgi?http://www.dod.mil/news/Mar2003/ n03262003_200303265.html.*

2 Aukofer and Lawrence, p. 46.

3 403 U.S. 713, 723–24 (J. Douglas, concurring).

4 403 U.S. 713, 723–24 (J. Douglas, concurring).

5 Ibid., p. 726–727 (J. Brennan, concurring).

6 Mark C. Rahdert, "The First Amendment and Media Rights During Wartime: Some Thoughts After Operation Desert Storm," 36 Villanova L. Rev. 1513, 1530 (1991).

7 Frank Aukoker and William Lawrence, "America's Team: The Odd Couple– A Report on the Relationship Between the Media and the Military," Freedom Forum, 1995, p. 3.

8 C. Robert Zelnick, "The Press and National Security: Military Secrets and First Amendment Values," 1 J. *National Security Law Journal* 21, 33 (1997).

9 *Branzburg* v. *Hayes*, 408 U.S. 665, 681 (1972).

10 Michael D. Steger, "Slicing the Golden Knot: A Proposal to Reform Military Regulation of Media Coverage of Combat Operations," 28 U.S.F. L. Rev. 957, 992–993 (1994).

11 Ibid., 991.

12 David A. Freznick, "The First Amendment on the Battlefield," 23 Pacific L.J. 315 (1992).

13 Robert O'Neil, "The Press and National Security," 1 *Journal of National Security Law* 1, 14 (1997).

Point: Cameras Distort Trial Proceedings and Should Be Prohibited

1 See Tony Mauro, "The Camera-Shy Federal Courts: Why Are Cameras Accepted in State Court but Dreaded in Federal Courts," *Media Studies Journal* (Winter 1998), p. 60–65.

2 *Sheppard* v. *Maxwell*, 384 U.S. 333, 343 (1966).

3 381 U.S. 532, 540 (1965).

4 Ibid. at 547.

5 Ibid. at 548.

6 Ibid. at 549.

7 Ibid.

8 *Chandler* v. *Florida*, 449 U.S. 560, 582 (1981).

9 Lassiter at p. 11.

10 Moussaoui, 205 F.R.D. at 185.

11 Ibid. at 185–186.

12 Ibid. at 186.

13 *Courtroom Television Network LLC* v. *State of New York*, 769 N.Y.S.2d 70 (N.Y. 2003), citing Public Papers of Governor Dewey, 324–325 (1952).

14 *Courtroom Television Network LLC* v. *State of New York*, 769 N.Y.S.2d 70, 86 (2003).

15 Gerald Uelman, *Lessons From the Trial: People* v. *O.J. Simpson,* Kansas City, MO: Andrews and McNeel, 1996, p. 92.

16 Ibid., p.94.

Counterpoint: Cameras in the Courtroom Enhance Public Knowledge of and Greater Credibility to Our Judicial System

1 *Richmond Newspapers, Inc.* v. *Virginia,* 448 U.S. 555 (1980).

2 Quoted in Ken Myers, "Professors Use People v. Simpson As Today's Educational Television," *The National Law Journal,* 2/6/1995, pg. A18.

3 Daniel Stepniak, "A Comparative Analysis of First Amendment Rights and the Televising of Court Proceedings," 40 Idaho L. Rev. 315, 322 (2004).

4 RTNDA, Freedom of Information: Cameras in the Court: A State-By-State Guide. Available online at *http://www.rtnda.org/foi/scc.html*.

5 Florida Rules of Judicial Administration Available online at *http://www.flabar .org/TFB/TFBResources.nsf/Attachments/63413B851B738BA585256B290 04BF86B/$FILE/04judadm.pdf? OpenElement.*

6 Fred Graham, "Doing Justice With Cameras in the Courtroom," in *Media Studies Journal: Covering the Courts* (Winter 1998), 32–37 at 34.

7 Ibid., p. 34–35.

8 Alan M. Dershowitz, *Reasonable Doubts,* New York: Simon & Schuster, 1996, p. 147–148.

9 Interview with Johnnie L. Cochran, "Lessons From the O.J. Simpson Trial II: The Camera Is the Defendants' Friend," in *Media Studies Journal: Covering the Courts* (Winter 1998), p. 45.

10 Ibid.

11 *Richmond Newspapers, Inc.* v. *Virginia,* 448 U.S. 555 (1980).

12 449 U.S. 560 (1981).

13 Ibid., p. 574.

14 Interview with Judge Richard S. Arnold and Judge Gilbert S. Merritt, "Justice by the Consent of the Governed," in *Media Studies Journal: Covering the Courts.*

Conclusion

1 *Sunshine & Secrecy: The Freedom of Information Act Turns 30* (Freedom Forum, 1996), p. 43.

2 Ibid., p. 41.

3 *American Civil Liberties Union v. Department of Defense,* No. 04 Civ. 4151 (AKH)(S.D.N.Y.)(9/15/04).

Books and Articles

Anderson, Keith. "Is There Still a Sound Legal Basis? The Freedom of Information Act in the Post 9/11 World," 64 Ohio St. L.J. 1605 (2003).

Bliss, Jeremy C. "The Press Goes to War," *Hoover Digest* (Summer 2003). Available online at *http://www.hooverdigest.org/033/bliss.html.*

Braverman, Burt A. and Frances J. Chetwynd. *Information Law: Freedom of Information Privacy Open Meetings Other Access.* New York: Practicing Law Institute, 1985.

Brenowitz, Stephanie. "Deadly Secrecy: The Erosion of Public Information Under Private Justice," 38 Ohio St. J. on Disp. Resol. 679 (2004).

Brill, Steven. "That's Entertainment! The Continuing Debate Over Cameras in the Courtroom," *Federal Lawyer.* July 1995.

DelVecchio, Brian William. "Press Access to American Military Operations and the First Amendment: The Constitutionality of Imposing Restrictions," 31 Tulsa L.J. 227 (1995).

Freedom Forum. "Sunshine & Secrecy: The Freedom of Information Act Turns 30," 1997.

Freedom Forum. Covering the Courts. *Media Studies Journal* (Winter 1998).

Freznick, David A. "The First Amendment on the Battlefield: A Constitutional Analysis of Press Access to Military Operations in Grenada, Panama and the Persian Gulf," 23 Pacific L.J. 315 (1992).

Hammitt, Harry A., David L. Sobel, and Mark S. Zaid, eds. *Litigation Under the Federal Open Government Laws 2002.* Las Vegas, NV: Epic Publications, 2002.

Hentoff, Nat. "Privacy, Shmivacy: We Need Cameras in Supreme Court," First Amendment Center Online, 12/02/03. Available online at *http://www.firstamendmentcenter.org/commentary.aspx?id=12293.*

Hoefges, Michael, Martin E. Halstuk, and Bill F. Chamberlain. "Privacy Rights Versus FOIA Disclosure Policy: The 'Uses and Effects' Double Standard in Access to Personally-Identifiable Information in Government Records," 12 *William & Mary Bill of Rights Journal* 1 (2003).

Johnson, Jeffrey S. "The Entertainment Value of a Trial: How Media Access to the Courtroom Is Changing the American Judicial Process," 10 Vill. Sports & Ent. L.J. 131 (2003).

Kelly, Carlos A. "The Pen is Mightier Than the Sword or Why the Media Should Exercise Self-restraint in Time of War," *Florida Bar Journal* (Jan. 2003).

Lassiter, Christo. "Put the Lens Cap Back on Cameras in the Courtroom: A Fair Trial Is At Stake," *New York State Bar Journal* (Jan. 1995).

Lee, Douglas. "Official Secrecy Helps Terrorists Undermine Democracy," First Amendment Center Online, 1/13/04. Available online at *http://www.firstamendmentcenter.org/commentary.aspx?id=12454.*

Lee, William E. "Security Review and the First Amendment," 25 Harv. J.L. & Pub. Pol'y 743 (2002).

Lemberg, James. "Pleading the First: The Public's First Amendment Right of Access to High-profile Trials Is at Risk, as More and More Judges Shield Court Proceedings From the News Media," *The News Media & the Law* (Spring 2004).

Loop, Travis. "Stepping Up Secrecy: The Delicate Balance of Press Freedom and National Security in the Post-Sept. 11 World," *Presstime* (September 2003), p. 34–41.

Mauro, Tony. "Supreme Court's Ruling Marks Blow to Public's Right to Know." *USA Today*, 4/6/04. Available online at *http://www.usatoday.com/news/opinion/editorials/2004-04-06-scotus-edit_x.htm.*

McLaughlin, James. "Blackout of Justice," *The News Media & the Law* (Winter 2004). Available online at *http://rcfp.org/news/mag/28-1/cov-blackout.html.*

McMasters, Paul K. "Denial of Access Shushes the Democratic Dialogue," First Amendment Center Online, 12/12/01. Available online at *http://www.firstamendmentcenter.org/commentary.aspx?id=15517.*

McMasters, Paul K. "Over-reaching Secrecy Undermines America's Safety," First Amendment Center Online, 6/20/04. Available online at *http://www.firstamendmentcenter.org/commentary.aspx?id=13538.*

Miller, Jennifer J. "Cameras in Courtrooms: The Lens of the Public Eye on Our System of Justice," *South Carolina Lawyer* (March/April 2002).

Muller, Eric L. "12/7 and 9/11: War Liberties and the Lessons of History," 104 W. Va. L. Rev. 571 (2002).

O'Neil, Robert M. "The Press and National Security: The Media and the Military: The Persian Gulf War and Beyond," 1 J. Nat'l Security L.J. 1 (1997).

Paulson, Ken. "Supreme Court Places a Premium on Privacy," First Amendment Center Online, 4/01/04. Available online at *http://www.firstamendmentcenter.org/commentary.aspx?id=13104.*

Reporters Committee for Freedom of the Press. Homefront Confidential: How the War on Terrorism Affects Access to Information and the Public's Right to Know. (4th ed.) Available online at *http://www.rcfp.org/home-frontconfidential/*.

Schoenhard, Paul M. "Disclosure of Government Information Online: A New Approach From an Existing Framework," 15 Harv. J. Law & Tech. 497 (2002).

Silverman, Matthew A. "National Security and the First Amendment: A Judicial Role in Maximizing Public Access to Information," 78 Ind. L.J. 1101 (2003).

Sinai, Karen C. "Shock and Awe: Does the First Amendment Protect a Media Right of Access to Military Operations," 22 Cardozo Arts & Ent. L.J. (2004).

Sloviter, Dolores K. "If Courts Are Open, Must Cameras Follow," 26 Hofstra L. Rev. 873 (1998).

Smith, Taffiny L. "The Distortion of Trials Through Televised Proceedings," 21 *Law & Psychology Rev.* 257 (1997).

Stepniak, Daniel. "The Comparative Analysis of First Amendment Rights and the Televising of Court Proceedings," 40 Idaho L. Rev. 315 (2004).

Taylor, Phillip and Lucy Dalglish. "How the U.S. Government Has Undermined Journalists' Ability to Cover the War on Terrorism," *Communications Lawyer* (Spring 2002).

Vladeck, David C. "Freedom of Information Overview," First Amendment Center Online. Available online at *http://www.firstamendmentcenter.org/press/information/overview.aspx*.

Zelnick, C. Robert. "The Press and National Security: Military Secrets and First Amendment Values," 1 J. Nat'l Security L. 21 (1997).

Websites

American Civil Liberties Union on FOIA
http://archive.aclu.org/library/foia.html.
The ACLU's book on FOIA entitled *Using the Freedom of Information Act: a Step-by-Step Guide.*

The Brechner Center for Freedom of Information
http://brechner.org/.
Based in Florida, this site contains information on FOIA issues with emphasis on Florida law.

California First Amendment Coalition
http://www.cfac.org/index.htm.
This site contains many resources on the public's right to know.

Center for Investigative Reporting, Inc.
http://www.muckraker.org/cir_info.php.
Websites for Investigative Reporters.

Electronic Privacy Information Center
http://www.epic.org/.
This site of advocacy group contains much information on FOIA.

First Amendment Center Online
http://www.firstamendmentcenter.org.
This site contains an overview of numerous First Amendment issues.

Freedom of Information Center, University of Missouri
http://foi.missouri.edu/.
This site contains an incredible amount of resources on FOIA issues.

John E. Moss Foundation
http://www.johnemossfoundation.org/.
Foundation named for John E. Moss, the father of the Freedom of Information Act.

The National Security Archive
http://www.gwu.edu/~nsarchiv/.
Based at George Washington University, this site contains volumes of information about FOIA and material released under FOIA.

Public Citizen's Freedom of Information Clearinghouse
http://www.citizen.org/litigation/free_info/.
Resource on FOIA by Public Citizen, a group devoted to public access.

Radio-Television News Directors Association & Foundation
http://www.rtnda.org/foi/scc.html.
This site contains state-to-state resources on camera access.

Reporters Committee for Freedom of the Press
http://www.rcfp.org.
This site of free-press advocacy group contains countless resources on open government issues, including the exhaustive study Homefront Confidential.

Society for Professional Journalists
http://www.spj.org.
This site for professional journalists contains information on press rights.

U.S. Department of Justice on FOIA
http://www.usdoj.gov/04foia/.
The Department of Justice's site devoted to FOIA.

Cases

***Campus Communications, Inc.* v. *Earnhardt*,** 821 So.2d 388 (Fla.App. 5th Dist. 2002).
Florida appeals court upholds state law barring release of autopsy photographs in case involving death of NASCAR legend Dale Earnhardt.

***Center for National Security Studies* v. *U.S. Department of Justice*,** 331 F.3d 918 (D.C. Cir. 2003).
Federal appeals court rejects FOIA and First Amendment challenges to release of names of 9/11 detainees and their attorneys.

***Chandler* v. *Florida*,** 449 U.S. 560 (1981).
U.S. Supreme Court rules that use of cameras in criminal trials does not per se violate due process rights of criminal defendants.

***Courtroom Television Network LLC* v. *State of New York*,** 769 N.Y.S.2d 70 (2003).
New York trial court opinion upholding state law banning camera access.

***Detroit Free Press* v. *Ashcroft*,** 303 F.3d 681 (6th Cir. 2002).
Federal appeals court rejects Creppy Memorandum and rules it violates the First Amendment.

***Estes* v. *Texas*,** 381 U.S. 532 (1965).
U.S. Supreme Court reverses criminal defendant's conviction, ruling that televising of trial contributed to violation of defendant's due-process rights.

***Flynt* v. *Rumsfeld*,** 355 F.3d 697 (D.C. Cir. 2004).
Federal appeals court rejects Larry Flynt's First Amendment right of access claims to the military battlefields in Afghanistan.

***Hartford Courant Company* v. *Pellegrino*,** No. 03-9141 (2nd Cir.)(6/8/04).
Federal appeals court recognizes public's qualified right of access to inspect court docket sheets.

***JB Pictures, Inc.* v. *Department of Defense*,** 86 F.3d 236 (D.C. Cir. 1996).
Federal appeals court upholds military ban on press access to returned caskets on military bases.

***National Archives and Records Administration* v. *Favish*,** 124 S.Ct. 1570 (2004).
U.S. Supreme Court decision that upholds government's denial of FOIA request to attorney investigating death of former White House lawyer Vince Foster.

***New Jersey* v. *Hauptmann*,** 115 N.J.L. 412 (1935).
New Jersey high court affirms kidnapper's conviction and rejects arguments that excessive media coverage violated defendant's constitutional rights.

***New York Times Co.* v. *United States*,** 403 U.S. 713 (1971).
Landmark U.S. Supreme Court decision that upholds right of press to publish secret documents about U.S. decision making with regards to entering the Vietnam War.

North Jersey Media Group **v.** *Ashcroft*, 308 F.3d 198 (3rd Cir. 2002).
Federal appeals court upholds Creppy Memorandum, banning access across-
the-board to all special interest immigration cases.

People **v.** *Kopp*, 756 N.Y.S.2d 830 (2003).
New York court upholds ban on camera access.

United States Department of Defense **v.** *Federal Labor Relations Authority*,
510 U.S. 487 (1994).
U.S. Supreme Court decision ruling that FOIA privacy exemption applies to
disclosure of home addresses to requesting unions.

United States Department of Justice **v.** *Reporters Committee for Freedom
of the Press*, 489 U.S. 1468 (1989).
U.S. Supreme Court applies FOIA privacy exemption to prevent disclosure of
FBI rap sheets.

U.S. **v.** *Moussaoui*, 205 F.R.D. 183 (E.D. Virg. 2002).
Federal district court upholds ban on camera access to trial of suspected terrorist.

Terms and Concepts

Compelling interest
Fair trial
First Amendment
Freedom of Information
National security
Open meetings
Open records
Prior restraint
Sixth Amendment
Strict scrutiny
Statute

Beginning Legal Research

The goal of POINT/COUNTERPOINT is not only to provide the reader with an introduction to a controversial issue affecting society, but also to encourage the reader to explore the issue more fully. This appendix, then, is meant to serve as a guide to the reader in researching the current state of the law as well as exploring some of the public-policy arguments as to why existing laws should be changed or new laws are needed.

Like many types of research, legal research has become much faster and more accessible with the invention of the Internet. This appendix discusses some of the best starting points, but of course "surfing the Net" will uncover endless additional sources of information—some more reliable than others. Some important sources of law are not yet available on the Internet, but these can generally be found at the larger public and university libraries. Librarians usually are happy to point patrons in the right direction.

The most important source of law in the United States is the Constitution. Originally enacted in 1787, the Constitution outlines the structure of our federal government and sets limits on the types of laws that the federal government and state governments can pass. Through the centuries, a number of amendments have been added to or changed in the Constitution, most notably the first ten amendments, known collectively as the Bill of Rights, which guarantee important civil liberties. Each state also has its own constitution, many of which are similar to the U.S. Constitution. It is important to be familiar with the U.S. Constitution because so many of our laws are affected by its requirements. State constitutions often provide protections of individual rights that are even stronger than those set forth in the U.S. Constitution.

Within the guidelines of the U.S. Constitution, Congress—both the House of Representatives and the Senate—passes bills that are either vetoed or signed into law by the President. After the passage of the law, it becomes part of the United States Code, which is the official compilation of federal laws. The state legislatures use a similar process, in which bills become law when signed by the state's governor. Each state has its own official set of laws, some of which are published by the state and some of which are published by commercial publishers. The U.S. Code and the state codes are an important source of legal research; generally, legislators make efforts to make the language of the law as clear as possible.

However, reading the text of a federal or state law generally provides only part of the picture. In the American system of government, after the legislature passes laws and the executive (U.S. President or state governor) signs them, it is up to the judicial branch of the government, the court system, to interpret the laws and decide whether they violate any provision of the Constitution. At the state level, each state's supreme court has the ultimate authority in determining what a law means and whether or not it violates the state constitution. However, the federal courts—headed by the U.S. Supreme Court—can review state laws and court decisions to determine whether they violate federal laws or the U.S. Constitution. For example, a state court may find that a particular criminal law is valid under the state's constitution, but a federal court may then review the state court's decision and determine that the law is invalid under the U.S. Constitution.

It is important, then, to read court decisions when doing legal research. The Constitution uses language that is intentionally very general—for example, prohibiting "unreasonable searches and seizures" by the police—and court cases often provide more guidance. For example, the U.S. Supreme Court's 2001 decision in *Kyllo* v. *United States* held that scanning the outside of a person's house using a heat sensor to determine whether the person is growing marijuana is unreasonable—*if* it is done without a search warrant secured from a judge. Supreme Court decisions provide the most definitive explanation of the law of the land, and it is therefore important to include these in research. Often, when the Supreme Court has not decided a case on a particular issue, a decision by a federal appeals court or a state supreme court can provide guidance; but just as laws and constitutions can vary from state to state, so can federal courts be split on a particular interpretation of federal law or the U.S. Constitution. For example, federal appeals courts in Louisiana and California may reach opposite conclusions in similar cases.

Lawyers and courts refer to statutes and court decisions through a formal system of citations. Use of these citations reveals which court made the decision (or which legislature passed the statute) and when and enables the reader to locate the statute or court case quickly in a law library. For example, the legendary Supreme Court case *Brown* v. *Board of Education* has the legal citation 347 U.S. 483 (1954). At a law library, this 1954 decision can be found on page 483 of volume 347 of the U.S. Reports, the official collection of the Supreme Court's decisions. Citations can also be helpful in locating court cases on the Internet.

Understanding the current state of the law leads only to a partial understanding of the issues covered by the POINT/COUNTERPOINT series. For a fuller understanding of the issues, it is necessary to look at public-policy arguments that the current state of the law is not adequately addressing the issue. Many groups lobby for new legislation or changes to existing legislation; the National Rifle Association (NRA), for example, lobbies Congress and the state legislatures constantly to make existing gun control laws less restrictive and not to pass additional laws. The NRA and other groups dedicated to various causes might also intervene in pending court cases: a group such as Planned Parenthood might file a brief *amicus curiae* (as "a friend of the court")—called an "amicus brief"—in a lawsuit that could affect abortion rights. Interest groups also use the media to influence public opinion, issuing press releases and frequently appearing in interviews on news programs and talk shows. The books in POINT/COUNTERPOINT list some of the interest groups that are active in the issue at hand, but in each case there are countless other groups working at the local, state, and national levels. It is important to read everything with a critical eye, for sometimes interest groups present information in a way that can be read only to their advantage. The informed reader must always look for bias.

Finding sources of legal information on the Internet is relatively simple thanks to "portal" sites such as FindLaw (*www.findlaw.com*), which provides access to a variety of constitutions, statutes, court opinions, law review articles, news articles, and other resources—including all Supreme Court decisions issued since 1893. Other useful sources of information include the U.S. Government Printing Office (*www.gpo.gov*), which contains a complete copy of the U.S. Code, and the Library of Congress's THOMAS system (*thomas.loc.gov*), which offers access to bills pending before Congress as well as recently passed laws. Of course, the Internet changes every second of every day, so it is best to do some independent searching. Most cases, studies, and opinions that are cited or referred to in public debate can be found online— and *everything* can be found in one library or another.

The Internet can provide a basic understanding of most important legal issues, but not all sources can be found there. To find some documents it is necessary to visit the law library of a university or a public law library; some cities have public law libraries, and many library systems keep legal documents at the main branch. On the following page are some common citation forms.

COMMON CITATION FORMS

Source of Law	Sample Citation	Notes
U.S. Supreme Court	*Employment Division* v. *Smith*, 485 U.S. 660 (1988)	The U.S. Reports is the official record of Supreme Court decisions. There is also an unofficial Supreme Court ("S. Ct.") reporter.
U.S. Court of Appeals	*United States* v. *Lambert*, 695 F.2d 536 (11th Cir.1983)	Appellate cases appear in the Federal Reporter, designated by "F." The 11th Circuit has jurisdiction in Alabama, Florida, and Georgia.
U.S. District Court	*Carillon Importers, Ltd.* v. *Frank Pesce Group, Inc.*, 913 F.Supp. 1559 (S.D.Fla.1996)	Federal trial-level decisions are reported in the Federal Supplement ("F. Supp."). Some states have multiple federal districts; this case originated in the Southern District of Florida.
U.S. Code	Thomas Jefferson Commemoration Commission Act, 36 U.S.C., §149 (2002)	Sometimes the popular names of legislation—names with which the public may be familiar—are included with the U.S. Code citation.
State Supreme Court	*Sterling* v. *Cupp*, 290 Ore. 611, 614, 625 P.2d 123, 126 (1981)	The Oregon Supreme Court decision is reported in both the state's reporter and the Pacific regional reporter.
State Statute	Pennsylvania Abortion Control Act of 1982, 18 Pa. Cons. Stat. 3203-3220 (1990)	States use many different citation formats for their statutes.

Images from Associated Press Graphics

DAVID L. HUDSON, JR., is an author-attorney who has published widely on First Amendment and other constitutional law issues. Hudson is a research attorney with the First Amendment Center at Vanderbilt and a First Amendment contributing editor to the American Bar Association's *Preview of United States Supreme Court Cases.* He obtained his undergraduate degree from Duke University and his law degree from Vanderbilt University Law School. This is his ninth book.

ALAN MARZILLI, M.A., J.D. of Durham, North Carolina, is an independent consultant working on several ongoing projects for state and federal government agencies and nonprofit organizations. He has spoken about mental health issues in thirty states, the District of Columbia, and Puerto Rico; his work includes training mental health administrators, nonprofit management and staff, and people with mental illness and their family members on a wide variety of topics, including effective advocacy, community-based mental health services, and housing. He has written several handbooks and training curricula that are used nationally. He managed statewide and national mental health advocacy programs and worked for several public interest lobbying organizations in Washington, D.C., while studying law at Georgetown University.